TWENTIETH CENTURY INTERPRETATIONS
OF
THE TRIAL

TWENTIETH CENTURY INTERPRETATIONS
OF
THE TRIAL

A Collection of Critical Essays

Edited by
JAMES ROLLESTON

Prentice-Hall, Inc.　　　　　*Englewood Cliffs, N. J.*

Library of Congress Cataloging in Publication Data
Main entry under title:

Twentieth century interpretations of The trial.

  (A Spectrum Book)
  Bibliography: p.
  1. Kafka, Franz, 1883-1924. Der Prozess.
I. Rolleston, James
PT2621.A26P78   833'.9'12 [B]   76-20816
ISBN 0-13-926345-4
ISBN 0-13-926337-3 pbk.

© 1976 by Prentice-Hall, Inc., Englewood Cliffs, New Jersey. A SPECTRUM BOOK. All rights reserved. No part of this book may be reproduced in any form or by any means without permission in writing from the publisher. Printed in the United States of America.

10 9 8 7 6 5 4 3 2 1

PRENTICE-HALL INTERNATIONAL, INC. (*London*)
PRENTICE-HALL OF AUSTRALIA PTY. LIMITED (*Sydney*)
PRENTICE-HALL OF CANADA, LTD. (*Toronto*)
PRENTICE-HALL OF INDIA PRIVATE LIMITED (*New Delhi*)
PRENTICE-HALL OF JAPAN, INC. (*Tokyo*)
PRENTICE-HALL OF SOUTHEAST ASIA PTE. LTD. (*Singapore*)
WHITEHALL BOOKS LIMITED, *Wellington, New Zealand*

*For Peter Demetz—
teacher and colleague extraordinary*

Contents

Introduction: On Interpreting *The Trial*   1
   by James Rolleston

Reading Kafka   11
   by Maurice Blanchot

Description of a Form   21
   by Martin Walser

The Role of Women   36
   by Wilhelm Emrich

The Legend of the Doorkeeper and Its Significance for Kafka's *Trial*   40
   by Ingeborg Henel

The Opaqueness of *The Trial*   56
   by Walter H. Sokel

Gesture and Posture as Elemental Symbolism in Kafka's *The Trial*   60
   by Karl J. Kuepper

Kafka and Phenomenology: Josef K.'s Search for Information   70
   by Cyrena N. Pondrom

Kafka's *The Trial*: The Semiotics of the Absurd   86
   by Thomas M. Kavanagh

Man Guilty   94
   by Erich Heller

The Question of Law, The Question of Writing   100
    by Stanley Corngold

Kafka's Principal Works and His Recorded Private Reading   105
Bibliography: The Trial *in English*   108

TWENTIETH CENTURY INTERPRETATIONS
OF
THE TRIAL

Introduction: On Interpreting The Trial

"To read Franz Kafka is to become a critic," declares R.G. Collins, and Kafka's works seem to compel such a response. His most striking stylistic development in the years following the writing of "The Judgment" in September 1912 lay in the direction of the parable: Kafka's ever more concise narrative structures, far from resisting interpretation through the mystery at their center, urge us to dissect them, to speculate on the more enigmatic links in the tight fictional chain. Indeed this need for interpretation is probably as close as we can get to the rhythm of Kafka's universe; the author himself usually offers the first readings of his own fictions, through the actual characters of the narrative who obsessively interpret their situations, and, sometimes, through a framing cast of characters whose interpretative activity opens up the parable's events to a related fictional realm lacking precisely that coherence which defines the parable itself. Two of Kafka's most famous parables, "Before the Law" and "An Imperial Message," were actually published by him in his collection *A Country Doctor* (1919). The act of publication would seem to confirm their existence as independent works of literature; yet the process of writing these parables, as far as can be told from the manuscripts, was inseparable from the writing of the larger works, *The Trial* and "The Great Wall of China" respectively, in which they are embedded. Evidently Kafka himself understood his parables on two different levels, as inviting interpretation both in themselves and as a summation of a larger story which is destined to remain a fragment.

The exemplary status as keys to a larger whole, to which both parables would seem entitled by the way in which they are presented, is however itself a source of further complications. "An Imperial Message" is supposed to be a transparent expression of an enduring relationship between the people and the emperor, a static embodiment of a static truth; yet the parable occupies a pivotal position in the story, when the narrator is moving from an evocation of the total unity of the Chinese people in the mighty endeavor of the Great Wall to a puzzled contemplation of their utter scepticism and fragmentation. The narrator simply stops; and the story, by remaining a fragment, impels the reader back to the parable itself which had so "precisely" embodied its meaning. The messenger pressing on with the words of the dead Emperor, unable to reach even the outskirts of the enormous kingdom's capital city—this story can no longer be treated as a disturbing yet gemlike enigma. The reader wants to ask why the messenger persists in his hopeless mission, in what sense the people acknowledge the Emperor's authority—questions the surrounding narrative has provoked without answering. With "Before the Law" the situation is a little different, first because the interpretative activity begins within the parable itself, in the thought of the man from the country, and also because within the novel it is offered not as a crystallization of what we are learning anyway but as a corrective to Josef K.'s erroneous understanding of the Court. Thus not only is the parable itself constituted by the combat of opposing interpretations (neither the doorkeeper nor the man from the country is in a position of insight); but the arguments about its meaning conducted by Josef K. and the priest are themselves merely extensions of the conflict within the parable. Given the priority of Josef K.'s perspective and his inherent inability to "think about himself" (as the Inspector exhorts him to do in the opening chapter), there is simply no space in the novel for an "objective" interpretative activity. "The Great Wall of China," by contrast, pretends to a tone of absolute "objectivity"; but the gradual disintegration of meaning following the formulation of the parable shows that this stance is no more tenable than the partisan posture of the speakers in *The Trial*.

An option open to the reader, which one exercises almost instinctively, is to interpret "Before the Law" in the light of the events of *The Trial* itself. Ingeborg Henel's important essay is the most thorough example of this approach, and she reaches reasonably clear conclusions: Josef K. should acknowledge his guilt and the man from the country should pass through the door, not in the hope of salvation, but because this is the only genuinely human possibility. Certainly an aura of meaning along these lines seems to surround the novel; yet Mrs. Henel is only able to achieve such clarity by opening up the text at all points to the explicit theological utterances of Kafka himself in his sketches and diaries. Not even the most diehard New Critic denies any more the legitimacy of such an approach, least of all in the case of Kafka: Since *The Trial* itself remains a fragment, not prepared for publication by the author, it is meaningless to draw a firm line between the novel itself as "art" and the rest of Kafka's manuscripts as mere ancillary material. So the objection to this interpretative move outward from the text is not methodological; rather, it traps the critic into distorting the complex relationship between Kafka the maker of texts and Kafka the self-interpreter. It is inherent in the rhythm of Kafka's finished texts that they simultaneously generate interpretations and limit (without denying) the validity of any single interpretation. The manuscripts reveal how Kafka deleted all passages that would render the "meaning" of a scene too explicit. This is not because Kafka loved puzzles and wanted to make his book "obscure," but because he distrusted his own interpretative activity. He was obsessed by the goal of total textual self-containment, and he left innumerable stories in a more or less fragmentary state because he could not reconcile this goal with the requirement of a fictional ending. Indeed Kafka was bitterly critical even of such masterpieces as "The Metamorphosis" and "In the Penal Colony" because he regarded the conclusions as somehow botched.

The point here is not to reinstate the division between an "aesthetic" fictional realm and some presumably less privileged level of discourse; as the last example suggests, to do that with sufficient logical stringency one would have to become Kafka himself: It would be a pointless exercise for the modern reader to try to expose the presumed weakness of the end of "Metamorphosis." What is essential is to remember that, however shrewd and suggestive Kafka's notes on ideas, on religion, on literature, or on his own feelings might be, they did not possess for him that binding Flaubertian precision to which only literature could aspire. It has often been remarked that a sufficiently skillful critic can find in Kafka's notes and diaries quotations to support completely opposed views about his work: In a recent critical survey of Kafka research Peter U. Beicken, for example, finds in Kafka's words justification for an interpretation of "Before the Law" antithetical to that of Ingeborg Henel. He argues that the message of the parable is that the man from the country should shed his obsession with the Law, which signifies a "parasitic guilt-ideology," and walk away, thereby asserting his identity as a free man. Now it does not follow that either Henel or Beicken is necessarily "wrong," or that Kafka contradicts himself. What has happened is that, because Kafka's actual works are hard to understand, readers have rummaged among his personal writings for "explanations," and then have endowed the selected passages with the kind of weight they would not think of countenancing with any other writer. For the fact is that the thought of any serious person will evolve, over a period of years, in ways that may set a later utterance in seeming contradiction with an earlier one, although in context a psychological continuity can be perceived. Because Kafka's life was so "hermetic" and the line between his personal writing and his literary activity so hard to draw, this simple human fact has often been overlooked. Moreover, the level on which all "contradictions" are resolved—namely the psychological continuity of the individual Franz Kafka—is precisely *not* the level at which literature comes into being, as Kafka himself repeatedly tells us. Writing in his diary on September 23, 1912, about the composition of "The Judgment" the previous night, he says he had "thoughts about Freud, of course." This "of course," with its implication that Kafka had diagnosed himself at the personal level far more effectively than any critic, not only calls into question interpretations of Kafka relying on psychological models; it suggests that *any* interpretative process that would dismantle the literary text into the influences, opinions, and experiences that constitute its raw material ignores the very element that makes literature what it is. Kafka endeavored to focus and concentrate the diversity of his being into a text that could elude the banal limitations of psychology. If we reverse the flow, seeking the "human" diversity through sheer fear of such "inhuman" concentration, we are committing the absurdity to which Jorge Luis Borges draws attention in "The Babylon Lottery." There, a society which has adopted the strictly stylized existence of the lottery analyzes and qualifies the dispositions of the lottery to the point where it speculates that there is no difference between the structure of the lottery and the random dictates of life itself; that, in short, the lottery (the text), as a system of laws, does not exist.

We must, then, maintain a steady gaze at the texts as texts, insisting that the only "reality" is the one constituted by their verbal structures: The problem with both the discussions of "Before the Law" mentioned above is that they answer questions, concerning issues like guilt or freedom, which the texts do not actually ask. At the same time we cannot escape into the "objective" haven of stylistic analysis: The texts uproot such objectivity, insisting on their role as generators of interpretation. How is such interpretation to be carried out? "There are two ways to miss the point of Kafka's works. One is to interpret them naturally, the other is the supernatural interpretation," says Walter Benjamin in his magisterial essay, first published in 1934. What he means by this is not that we should rule out either "natural" or "supernatural" dimensions in our discussion of Kafka (to do so indeed would be to fall silent, a course the reader often finds tempting), but that we must reject all systematic "explanations" of the events in a Kafka text, whether these explanations derive from common sense or from theological allegory. For what Kafka has done as a writer is to fuse into a unique literary style all the discrete elements of the modern experience—from the unconscious to the refinements of metaphysical analysis, from the banal to the apocalyptic—elements which in our daily life are fragmented and incoherent, although never wholly absent. In *The Trial* Kafka welds into a continuous associative chain the daily bureaucratic routine of Josef K.; the stylizations of a court of law; and the primitive, almost superstitious level of existence at which humanity, fearing the chaotic freedom of its own consciousness, generated the notion of Law in the first place. A similar chain links the formal relationship between men and women in the post-Victorian era; the animal savagery of desire which the formalities are designed to check; and, in the figure of Leni, the archetypal imagery of dissolution and loss of self which the primitive (male) version of the world, conditioned by fear, has always assigned to women. Thus the "bottomlessness" which the reader senses when confronted by almost any sentence of *The Trial* derives not only—indeed not primarily—from the psychological complexity of Josef K. Kafka has established the narrative perspective at a point very close to the vision of his protagonist, but *not* in order to devalue the world of the novel into something secondary like Josef K.'s dream or private obsession. The famous sentence at the beginning of "The Metamorphosis"—"It was no dream"—echoes through all of Kafka's subsequent writing. Although it appears, and in "Before the Law" it is explicitly stated, that this fiction is intended solely for Josef K., clarity on this issue provides no more than the vantage point from which the novel's true obscurities can be discerned. For at the same time that Kafka establishes a single human perspective through which the action is exclusively articulated, he is insistently asking, both through the activity of the Court and through the ghostly presence of a narrator who undermines each and every one of Josef K.'s certainties, fundamental questions about his hero's existence. Josef K. is "everyman" only in the sense that, in the specific crisis of modern consciousness diagnosed by Kafka, the very concept of "man" is called into question. Heir to both the confident humanistic psychology of nineteenth-century realism and the terrifyingly destructive version of that same psychology found in writers like Kleist and Dostoevsky, Kafka explores throughout his literary career the strange and reductive conflict underlying every phase of human existence. That man exists seems subjectively undeniable, he thinks, speaks, affects others, and tirelessly insists on his own identity; at the same time he is incapable of constituting that identity rationally, for the smallest function of his daily life crumbles into meaninglessness upon examination, leaving only "the impossibility of living" (a phrase from Kafka's earliest work, "Description of a Struggle"). What man is most adept at doing is aligning himself with the quasi-ethical abstractions with which his subjectivity feels comfortable—in the case of Josef K., the word "innocence." Martin Walser has diagrammed the rhythm of *The Trial* according to the thesis that Kafka's novels are exclusively devoted to portraying the inflation and deflation of man's illusory assertions of identity. Walser rests his case with the assertion that the meaning of this literary enterprise is "meaninglessness."

And yet the reader stirs discontentedly at this conclusion, sensing, like Josef K. himself at the end of his debate with the priest about the parable, that this cannot be the "last word." The notion of meaning simply cannot be that easily disposed of: If it is absent, then there must be some context to that absence, some framework in which the word "meaning" has both an origin and a future. At the very moment when one's interpretative activity is directed towards a bleak reductiveness like Walser's, the richness of Kafka's texts compels one to pause, to rephrase one's own questions. (Walser himself stands back from his interpretation and formulates a theory connecting Kafka with the epic tradition.) This is not to say that the text is "obscure,"—describable only through a multiplicity of conflicting interpretations. Nothing could be more precise than Kafka's language. The problem is simply that the text cannot be translated directly into, or even adequately evoked by, any other terminology. One's image of this situation should be vertical rather than lateral: The text is situated on a particular linguistic level at which only its own language is adequate. However, there are realms above it (religious consciousness) and below it (instinct and ancient custom) to which the text is constantly alluding. The interpreter's task is to range freely in and between these realms, intersecting with the text en route, locating the models (religion, literature, ritual, theater, etc.) on which a particular text has drawn for its organization. This kind of "vertical" criticism, enlarging the work's resonance while refusing to confine it within any fixed frame of reference —even that of Kafka's own notes—is practiced to perfection by Walter Benjamin. There is no way to summarize his argument, which focuses simultaneously on the frozen stylization of the human gesture and the fluid undertow of man's most ancient fears and drives. The essay is a series of critical arabesques, taking off from the text in search of the "precursors" Kafka has made for himself (a theme later crystallized by Borges in "Kafka and his Precursors"), only to return to Kafka's words from a new vantage point. Despite the inevitable distortion, it is perhaps worthwhile to draw together passages nearly ten pages apart in Benjamin's essay in order to evoke the diversity of insight which he achieves.

"Like El Greco, Kafka tears open the sky behind every gesture; but as with El Greco—who was the patron saint of the Expressionists—the gesture remains the decisive thing, the center of the event. . . . Kafka did not consider the age in which he lived as an advance over the beginnings of time. His novels are set in a swamp world. In his works, created things appear at the stage which Bachofen has termed the hetaeric stage. The fact that it is now forgotten does not mean that it does not extend into the present. On the contrary: it is actual by virtue of this very oblivion."

Kafka's simultaneous probing of the heights of the cosmos and the depths of the swamp does not often emerge on the surface of his novels. When it does, as in the unfathomable glimpses vouchsafed to the hero at the end of both "Before the Law" and the novel itself, the reader, who has been trapped for long stretches within the arid self-justifications of the hero's consciousness, immediately turns back the pages, recasting what he has read, transcending Josef K.'s limitations. And in this way he becomes aware of a crucial source of the novel's power: *The Trial* is only able to occupy a privileged linguistic level, resisting translation into other terms, because it is itself constituted by a quest for that level of precision. Josef K. is the first "reader" of his own story; the actual events hardly exist prior to his interpretation of them (indeed he himself reflects in the course of the first chapter that a different response on his part would have stopped the trial in its tracks). The "center" of the work comes into being through Josef K.'s paradigmatic failure to achieve it. Moreover, Josef K.'s errors of interpretation correspond rather closely to the "supernatural" and "natural" approaches which Benjamin sees as underlying most Kafka criticism.

On the one hand, Josef K. strives for total comprehension of his situation, incessantly subordinating all details to a scheme of things intelligible to his reason; and in its willingness to adopt the trappings and categories of a legal system the Court encourages him to do this, since in any society the law represents man's most ambitious attempt to include all the possibilities of living in an unchanging code. On the other hand, Josef K. is easily deflected from this perspective into a helpless absorption in the specific details of any given situation in which he finds himself, studying the reactions of others the way the man from the country studies the fleas in the doorkeeper's collar. The Inspector's charge, in the first chapter, that Josef K. is insensitive to the nuances of his situation, indicates that the Court appears to encourage this attitude also. That both approaches are doomed to perpetual inadequacy—that they pass almost mathematically above and below the target of meaning at which Josef K. is aiming—becomes very clear in the Interrogation chapter when K. deploys both simultaneously and with great intensity: While his words are articulating "legal" verities, K. nervously analyses the reactions of his bizarre audience. This scene culminates in one of the "purest," least ambiguous failures in the whole work.

Obviously Josef K. will not achieve a center of meaning by these tactics; but equally obviously we cannot expect anything different from him, nor can we expect any change in the Court's behaviour, since this is "his" story and his alone, with the Court's strategy tailor-made to fit his experience, his assumptions, his weaknesses. The circle is complete: The novel's meaning is located in Joseph K.'s failure to achieve that meaning, yet "success" is inconceivable, since the premise of the novel is that its structure is generated by K. alone. However, a way into this circle is opened by the presence of a narrator who never becomes "independent" of Josef K. yet is not identical with him either. At the very moment that K. is interpreting his own story, along lines that ensure failure, his interpretation is itself being judged, not by the Court, which as we have seen tends to reinforce error, but by the narrator, through the intricate texture of subjunctive mood and parenthetical observation which constitutes Kafka's language. What I have called the "vertical" style of interpretation gains its justification from the sense that a vast segment of human history and literary experience is compressed into a single sentence of a Kafka text. What I would now designate as the "linear" approach seizes on the feeling, implied by the narrator's presence, that judgment is not meaningless, however complete the deterministic relationship between Josef K. and his story. Into the rhythm of inevitable negation, Kafka builds a counter-rhythm based on that Heideggerian quality of functional wholeness which is present in the very words he uses and which the narrator almost playfully indulges: Although the conception of the work precludes a "correct" or harmonious response by K., the inherent movement of language towards meaning and coherence prevents that possibility from being absent from the text. Even though the reader "knows" that Josef K. will always fail, he is not wrong to judge K. for his failure and to keep alive the sense that the theorem on which the novel is based may suddenly, at the thousandth testing, be proved wrong. And in the final chapter, K. delivers a judgment on himself corresponding closely to what the reader has been thinking. Of course, it would have been impossible for him to have achieved this insight earlier; and yet . . . even as the interpretative activity of the novel folds in on itself, methodically including all possibilities, the language of Kafka reaches out to the reader, acknowledging his existence as a human being capable of eluding the text's determinism.

A linear interpretation is beset by far more pitfalls than a vertical one. For the latter, what is needed is a combination of audacity, learning, and unwavering respect for the integrity of the text. A linear approach, however, since it gains access to the text through the position of the narrator, can never stray far from that position. If it does it will almost certainly fall prey to the errors committed by K. himself and by so many critics since. On the one side the interpreter is very likely to grow impatient with the tortuous movement of the text and to begin selecting "key" passages; from there to a static "explanation" of Josef K.'s behavior and the Court's intentions is only a short step, yet it is one that fatally violates both the self-enclosure and the restless motion of the text. An even greater temptation is to overcompensate for this danger by delving into the subtlest nuances, the almost invisible details of each individual sentence. This approach is not without prospects for ultimate success, just as it is not theoretically impossible for Josef K. to write an account of his entire life. One thinks of those editions of Dante and Shakespeare containing ten lines of notes for every single line of text. Yet should Kafka ever be blessed (or cursed) by such an edition, the interpretative problem will not have been solved, any more than it has been solved for Dante or Shakespeare. The larger rhythm, the life of the work, cannot be reached through a process of endless analysis and subdivision; the center will withhold itself from such criticism, just as it withholds itself from the man from the country, and from Josef K. himself.

Even if a linear critic avoids these pitfalls, the narrowness of the aperture (the narrator's presence) through which he gains access ensures that he is never free of a third danger—that of simply reproducing the text. Borges' Pierre Menard (How often Borges' name seems entwined with the problems of Kafka interpretation!), after years of intensively studying Cervantes' *Don Quixote*, finally produced his masterpiece: a word-for-word recomposition of the original. And yet a linear interpretation, in search of the specific rhythms, the recurring models by means of which Kafka has brought Josef K. and his world into being, cannot leave anything out of account. It must be a "close reading" in the fullest sense of the word, introducing from Kafka's personal writings only such comments as seem linguistically related to the novel, and refraining—as Kafka himself so carefully refrained—from using them to "explain" the text. Only thus can justice be done to the artistic perfectionism Kafka imposed on himself. Does this mean that we have to treat Kafka's texts as "sacred?" The analogy is quite apt and the answer is that there is simply no alternative. Kafka would have been happy for posterity to forget him; but since he has become and remains important to us, we must approach him on his own terms—as a writer of fictions—and not as a prophet, a neurotic, or a social commentator. But it is precisely the analogy with sacred texts that ensures we do not have to fall silent. For sacred texts exist in order to be interpreted, and there is no limit to the directions in which one may move in order to collect information about them. A great deal is known about Kafka, about his family life, his social and religious views, his relations with women (particularly since the publication of the *Letters to Felice*), and his literary ancestry (The little table at the end of this volume of authors' names as recorded in Kafka's diaries and letters is designed to offer food for thought along these lines). All of this can be usefully sifted and absorbed by the critic before confronting the central mysteries of the works themselves; but such knowledge is no guarantee that the critic will achieve better insights into the texts than the student approaching them for the first time. The principal asset the interpreter of Kafka can bring to his task is a full awareness of his position as a free man over against the imprisoned creatures of the fictional world, and, conversely, as one whose understanding, however well articulated, will resound for only a short while before being absorbed with hardly a trace in the restless silence of the text.

To call a selection of essays on *The Trial* arbitrary would be an understatement. The basic decision I have taken is to offer general reflections on the text as a whole rather than detailed studies of particular motifs or contexts, valuable though such work can be. To offset this omission I have provided an extensive bibliography of writing in English or English translation on *The Trial*. Three pieces, those by Blanchot, Walser and Henel, appear here in English for the first time; all are of established significance in the history of Kafka criticism. The essay by Stanley Corngold, an important figure in contemporary Kafka studies, was written especially for this volume; and the essays by Pondrom and Kavanagh are especially interesting as providing bridges between Kafka criticism, with its understandable tendency towards introversion, and the most productive trends in modern literary analysis.

It should be stressed that there is no standard pagination of *The Trial* in English to which critics might refer. To follow up quotations from the novel, readers should check the edition named in each individual article.

Permission to quote from Franz Kafka's writings is acknowledged as follows:

The Trial, reprinted by permission of Schocken Books Inc. and Alfred A. Knopf. Copyright 1937, © 1956 by Alfred A. Knopf. Copyright renewed 1965 by Alfred A. Knopf Inc.

Excerpts from *Dearest Father* are reprinted by permission of Schocken Books Inc. from *Dearest Father* by Franz Kafka. Copyright 1954 by Schocken Books Inc.

Excerpts from *Diaries 1910–1913* are reprinted by permission of Schocken Books Inc. from *Diaries 1910–1913* by Franz Kafka. Copyright © 1948 by Schocken Books, Inc.

Excerpts from *Diaries 1914–1923* are reprinted by permission of Schocken Books Inc. from *Diaries 1914–1923* by Franz Kafka. Copyright © 1949 by Schocken Books Inc.

Excerpts from *The Trial* (Canada only) are reprinted by permission of Schocken Books Inc. from *The Trial* by Franz Kafka. Copyright 1937, © 1956 by Alfred A. Knopf, Inc. Copyright renewed 1964 by Alfred A. Knopf, Inc.

Excerpts from *Letters to Felice* reprinted by permission of Schocken Books Inc. from *Letters to Felice* by Franz Kafka. Copyright © 1967, 1973 by Schocken Books Inc.

Permission to quote from the works listed above has also been granted by Martin Secker and Warburg Ltd., London.

Reading Kafka

by Maurice Blanchot
translated by Glenn W. Most

Perhaps the reason Kafka wanted to destroy his literary works was that they seemed to him condemned to increase universal misunderstanding.[1] When we observe the disorder in which these works are rendered[2] to us, and what in them we are made to understand and what is concealed from us; the partial light which is projected onto one fragment or another; the dispersion of texts which are themselves incomplete to begin with and which are divided further and further, or even reduced to powder (as though they were relics whose inherent virtue were indivisible)—when one sees these fundamentally silent works invaded by the idle chatter of

---

"La Lecture de Kafka," from *La Part du feu* (Paris: Gallimard, 1949), pp. 9–19. Copyright © 1949 by Editions Gallimard. The reader is, in general, warned that Blanchot's French is characterized by untranslatable ambiguity. The preposition in the title, for example, seems primarily to operate as an objective genitive, referring to the experience of the reader confronting the texts of Kafka, and has been so translated here in order to emphasize the degree to which Blanchot is concerned with developing a general theory of reading. But latent within the title lies another possibility: a subjective genitive, referring to Kafka's own experience in reading—that is, to the conflict between Kafka in his relation to the world and Kafka in his relation to literature, a conflict which is a recurrent theme in the writings of Blanchot, who claims repeatedly that the author is only capable of creating a work of literature insofar as he effaces himself as a man. Compare Martin Heidegger: "Precisely in great art—and I speak here only of great art—the artist remains something indifferent with regard to the work, almost like a passage for the coming into existence of the work, a passage which destroys itself in the act of creation." "Der Ursprung des Kunstwerkes," in *Holzwege*, 5th edition (Frankfurt am Main: Vittorio Klostermann, 1972), p. 29. I wish to acknowledge the assistance of D. Glassman and C. Larmore in preparing this translation.

[1] The plural "works" translates the singular French "oeuvre," and does so here with an unusual appropriateness: for the danger, which might be offered by the singular, of totalizing all of an author's individual texts into a single homogeneous one, is one that Blanchot himself explicitly attempts to avoid (note his stress, for example, at the beginning of the eleventh paragraph, on the incompleteness and fragmentation of Kafka's writings).

[2] I have attempted to convey by the English "rendered," a pun in Blanchot's "livrée." Although the French word means literally "to deliver" or "to betray," it contains also within it the word for book ("livre"), and hence implies one of Blanchot's dominant themes: the contrast between the inaccessibility of an author's authentic literary discourse and the inauthenticity of that discourse once it falls into the public domain of ordinary language.

commentaries or, unpublishable themselves, made into material for infinite publications—a timeless creation changed into a gloss on history—then one begins to wonder whether Kafka himself foresaw such a disaster within such a triumph. Perhaps his desire was to disappear, discreetly, like an enigma which wants to escape our gaze. But this discretion rendered him to the public, this secret made him glorious. Now the enigma is displayed in shop windows everywhere: It is the very daylight, it is its own theatrical production. What is to be done?

Kafka's *Diary* proves to us that he never wanted to be anything other than a writer; but the *Diary* ends up by showing us in Kafka something more than a writer: It gives precedence to the man who lived over the man who wrote; and it is the former we shall seek henceforth in his works. These works form the scattered remains of an existence which they help us to understand: They are the invaluable witness of an extraordinary destiny which, without them, would have remained unseen. Perhaps it is the peculiarity of books like *The Trial* and *The Castle* that they refer us endlessly to an extra-literary truth which we begin to betray at the very moment that it lures us out of the literature with which this truth can not, however, merge.

This movement is inevitable. All the commentators implore us to look for narratives within these narratives: The events signify nothing but themselves, the surveyor really is a surveyor. Do not substitute "dialectical constructions for the unfolding of events that must be construed as a realistic narrative" (Claude-Edmonde Magny). But several pages further on: One can "find in the works of Kafka a theory of responsibility, views concerning causality, finally a comprehensive interpretation of the human condition, all three sufficiently coherent and independent enough of their novelistic form to survive transposition into purely intellectual terms." This contradiction might seem bizarre. And it is true that these texts have often been translated [3] with a peremptory decision, with an evident scorn for their artistic character. But it is also true that Kafka himself set a precedent by sometimes providing commentaries for his stories and by seeking to elucidate their meaning. The difference, however, is that, with the exception of a few details whose genesis (rather than signification) he explains to us, he does not transpose the narrative onto a level which might make it easier for us to grasp: The language he uses as commentator buries itself within the fiction and does not distinguish itself from it.

The *Diary* is filled with remarks which seem to be bound to an easily recognizable mode of theoretical discourse. But these thoughts remain

---

[3] As is clear from the context, the French "traduit" is to be understood here as referring to an activity of interpretation rather than to that which is usually meant by translation; but, by using this word, Blanchot sharpens his critique of an interpretation which would consist merely in the quasi-allegorical transposition of Kafka's writings from one mode of discourse entirely into another.

foreign to the level of generality whose form they borrow. It is as though they are in exile there: They fall back into an equivocal modality which allows them to be understood neither as the expression of a unique event nor as the explication of a universal truth. The thought of Kafka can not be related to a uniformly valid rule, but just as little does it derive from simple reference to particular facts of his life. It hovers between these alternatives.[4] As soon as it becomes the transposition of a series of events which have really occurred (as is the case in a diary), it passes imperceptibly into a search for the meaning of those events; it desires to approach them more closely. It is then that the narrative begins to coalesce with its explication: But the explication is not an explication of the narrative; it does not arrive at what it seeks to explain, and above all it does not succeed in attaining a vantage point from which to survey it. It is as though it were drawn, by its own weight, toward the particularity whose closed character it must break apart. The meaning it sets in motion wanders around the facts: And although it can become an explication only if it succeeds in detaching itself from them, it remains an explication only—if indeed it is inseparable from them. Reflection's infinite meanderings, its returns to the starting-point of an image which shatters it, the scrupulous rigor of a reasoning process applied to a non-object: These constitute the modalities of a thought which plays at generalizing but which is only thought insofar as it is caught within the density of a world reduced to the particular.

Mme. Magny remarks that Kafka never writes a platitude; and this not by an extreme refinement of intelligence, but instead by a sort of congenital indifference to received ideas. The thought of Kafka is indeed rarely banal, but the reason is that neither is it altogether a thought. It is singular, that is, exactly suited to only one person: Even if it makes use of abstract terms like positive, negative, good, evil, it still bears more resemblance to a strictly individual history[5] whose moments would be obscure events that, never yet having been produced, will never be reproduced. Kafka, in his autobiographical essay, described himself as a collection of particularities, some of which were secret, others declared, incessantly running foul of the norm and able neither to make themselves recognized nor to suppress themselves. This is a conflict the depths of whose meaning Kierkegaard sounded; but Kierkegaard took the side of the secret, while Kafka cannot take either side. If he conceals that part of himself which is bizarre, then he detests himself and his destiny, considering himself evil or damned; if he projects his secret outwards, that secret is not recognized by society, which returns it to him and reimposes it upon him.

[4] In French: "Elle est une nage fuyante entre ces deux eaux."
[5] The French "histoire" means both "history," in the sense of a connected series of events occurring over time, and "story," in the sense of the linguistic narration of those events.

Allegory, symbol, mythic fiction—those modes of discourse whose extraordinary developments are revealed to us by his works—are made indispensable for Kafka by the character of his meditation. This latter oscillates between the two poles of solitude and the law, of silence and ordinary language. It can attain neither the one nor the other, and this oscillation is at the same time an attempt to escape from oscillation. His thought can not find rest in the general; but, although it complains sometimes of its madness and of its confinement, it is nonetheless not absolute solitude, for it speaks of this solitude; it is not nonsense, for it has this nonsense for its sense; it is not outside the law, for its law is this banishment which already reconciles it. One can say of the absurd (which one might wish to make the measure of this thought) what Kafka himself says of the tribe of woodlice: "Try only to make yourself understood by the woodlouse: if you get to the point of asking it the purpose of its work, you will by the same token have exterminated the tribe of woodlice." At the moment thought encounters the absurd, this encounter signifies the end of the absurd.

Thus, all the texts of Kafka are condemned to recounting something unique and to seeming to recount it only in order to express its general signification. The narrative is thought which has become a series of unjustifiable and incomprehensible events; and the meaning which haunts the narrative is the same thought pursuing itself across the incomprehensible like the common sense which overturns it. He who remains at the level of the story penetrates into something opaque of which he cannot give an account; and he who holds to the meaning cannot rejoin the obscurity to which it draws attention like a beacon. The two readers can never catch up with one another: One is first one, then the other; one understands always more or always less than is necessary. The true reading remains impossible.

Whoever reads Kafka is thus necessarily transformed into a liar, and yet not entirely into a liar. It is there that the anxiety inherent in this art resides—an anxiety which is certainly more profound than the anguish concerning our fate of which Kafka's writings seem often to be the thematic expression. We fall immediately into a false position which we imagine we can avoid: We struggle against it (by the juxtaposition of contrary interpretations), and this effort is delusory; we consent to it, and this weakness is treason. Subtlety, cunning, candor, loyalty, negligence are all equally the means of an error (of a fraud) which lies within the truth of the words, within their exemplary power, within their clarity, their interest, their assurance, their power to draw us on, to abandon us, to take us up again, in that enduring belief in their meaning which permits one neither to fail it nor to follow it.

How are we to represent for ourselves this world which escapes us, not because it can not be grasped, but because on the contrary there is perhaps too much to grasp? The commentators do not even fundamentally disagree with one another. They all use almost exactly the same words: absurdity, contingency, the will to make a place for oneself in the world, the impossibility of maintaining oneself there, the desire of God, the absence of God, despair, anguish. And yet of whom are they speaking? For some, Kafka is a religious thinker who believes in the absolute, who even hopes for it, who in any event struggles endlessly to attain it. For others, he is a humanist who lives in a world without recourse and who, in order not to increase its disorder, remains, as far as possible, at rest. According to Max Brod, Kafka found many exits toward God. According to Mme. Magny, Kafka finds his principal source of strength in atheism. For another, there is certainly a world beyond, but it is inaccessible, perhaps evil, perhaps absurd. For another, there is neither a beyond nor a movement towards it; we are within immanence, what counts is the ever-present feeling of our finitude and the unresolved enigma to which it reduces us. Jean Starobinski: "A man struck by a bizarre evil, such is the way Franz Kafka appears to us. . . . Here a man sees himself devoured." And Pierre Klossowski: "The *Diary* of Kafka is . . . the diary of a sick man who desires to be healed. He wants health . . . thus he believes in health." And the same again: "In any case we can not speak of him as though he had not had a final vision." And Starobinski ". . . there is no last word, there can be no last word."

These texts reflect the discomfort of a reading which seeks to preserve both the enigma and the solution, both the misunderstanding and the expression of this misunderstanding, the possibility of reading within the impossibility of interpreting this reading. Even ambiguity does not satisfy us: Ambiguity is a subterfuge which seizes the truth in the mode of slippage, of passage; yet the truth which awaits these writings is perhaps unique and simple. It is not certain that one understands Kafka better if against each affirmation one opposes an affirmation which upsets it, if one nuances infinitely the themes by means of others which are differently oriented. The law of contradiction does not reign in this world which excludes faith but not the search for faith, hope but not the hope for hope, truth here and beyond but not the appeal to an absolutely final truth. It is quite true that to explain such works by referring to the historical and religious condition of the man who wrote them, making of him a sort of greater Max Brod, is a highly unsatisfactory sleight-of-hand; but it is also true that if his myths and his fictions have no link with the past, their meaning refers us nevertheless to elements which this past elucidates, to problems which would certainly never have been posed in the same way if they were not already theological, religious, impregnated by the lacerated spirit of the unhappy consciousness. It is for this reason that, although one can be equally troubled by all the interpretations which are proposed to us, one can nevertheless not say that they are all valid, that they are all equally true or equally false, indifferent to their object or true only in their disagreement with one another.

The principal narratives of Kafka are fragments; the totality of his works is a fragment. This lack might explain the uncertainty which makes the form and the content of their reading unstable without changing their direction. But this lack is not accidental. It is incorporated within the very sense that it mutilates; it coincides with the representation of an absence which is neither tolerated nor rejected. The pages we read have the most extreme plenitude: They proclaim a work for which nothing is lacking; and, moreover, the whole of Kafka's works is, as it were, given in any one of these intricately unfolding narratives which interrupt themselves brusquely, as if there were nothing more to say. They lack nothing, not even that lack which is their object: It is not a lacuna; it is, rather, the sign of impossibilities which are present everywhere and are never admitted—the impossibility of communal existence, the impossibility of solitude, the impossibility of enduring these impossibilities.

What makes our effort to read anguishing is not the coexistence of different interpretations: It is, for each theme, the mysterious possibility of its appearing at one time with a negative and at another with a positive meaning. This world is a world of hope and a world condemned, a universe forever closed and a universe without limit, one of injustice and one of sin. What Kafka himself says of religious knowledge—"Such knowledge is at one and the same time both a passage leading to eternal life and an obstacle raised against that life"—must be said of his own works: Everything there is an obstacle, but everything there can also become a passage. Few texts are more sombre; and yet even those whose conclusion is without hope remain ready to reverse themselves in order to express an ultimate possibility, a neglected triumph, the radiance of an aspiration beyond fulfillment. By dint of deepening negativity, he gives it a chance of becoming positive—one chance only—a chance which is never entirely realized and across which its contrary never ceases to disclose itself.

All the works of Kafka are in search of an affirmation which they wish to acquire by negation, an affirmation which, the moment it appears in outline, eludes one's grasp, reveals itself as falsehood, and thus excludes itself from affirmation—thereby making affirmation once again possible. It is for this reason that it seems so curious to say of such a world that it does not know transcendence. Transcendence is precisely that affirmation which can only be affirmed by negation. By the very fact that it is denied, it exists; by the very fact that it is not there, it is present. God, having died, has found in these works a sort of terrifying revenge. For his death deprives him neither of his power, nor of his infinite authority, nor of his infallibility: Dead, he is only more terrible, more invulnerable—locked in a combat in which there is no longer any possibility of defeating him. It is with a dead transcendence that we are at grips: It is a dead emperor whom the bureaucrat of "The Great Wall of China" represents; it is, in "In the Penal Colony," the dead former commander whom the torture machine makes always present. And, as J. Starobinski remarks, is not the supreme judge of *The Trial* himself dead—he who is capable only of condemning to death—because it is death that is his power; death, and not life, that is his truth?

The ambiguity of the negative is linked to the ambiguity of death. "God is dead" is a statement that can signify this truth which is even harder to accept: "Death is not possible." In the course of a brief narrative entitled "The Hunter Gracchus," Kafka recounts for us the adventure of a hunter in the Black Forest who, having succumbed to a fall into a ravine, has nevertheless not succeeded in reaching the world beyond—and now he is both living and dead. He had joyously accepted life and joyously accepted the end of his life; once he had been killed, he awaited his death with joy: He lay outstretched and he waited. "Then," says Kafka, "came the mishap." This mishap is the impossibility of death; it is the derision, the night, the nothingness, the silence, all of those elements which are cast upon the great human subterfuges. There is no end, there is no possibility of ending one's obsession with the day, with the meanings of things, with hope: Such is the truth from which Western man has made a symbol of felicity. This is the truth which he has sought to make endurable by exposing its fortunate slope: the slope of immortality, of a survival that would compensate life. But this survival is, in fact, our very life. "After the death of a man," says Kafka, "a particularly beneficent silence intervenes for a short time on earth with respect to the dead: a terrestrial fever has found its end, one no longer sees a dying in process, an error seems to be corrected, even for the living it is an opportunity to catch their breath—that is why one opens the window of the mortuary chamber—until this easing of the situation appears illusory and pain and lamentations begin."

Kafka says elsewhere: "Lamentations at the death-bed have as object, in sum, the fact that the dead man is not dead in the true meaning of the word. We must still content ourselves with this way of dying: we continue to play the game." And this, which is just as clear: "Our salvation is death, but not this one." We do not die—that is the truth. But the result is that we do not live either: We are dead during our lifetime; we are essentially survivors. Thus death finishes our life, but it does not finish our possibility of dying; as the end of life it is real, but as the end of death it is only apparent. Hence that equivocation, that double equivocation which gives an air of strangeness to the slightest gestures of all these characters. Are they, like the hunter Gracchus, the dead who are futilely ceasing to die, beings who have been dissolved in unknown waters and whom the error of their former death maintains—with the smirk that suits death but also with its softness, its infinite courtesy—within the familiar decor of obvious reality? Or are they the living who, not comprehending, struggle with great dead enemies, with something which is finished and which is not finished, to which they give renewed existence by repelling it, and which they displace by the very activity of seeking it out? For here is the origin of our anxiety. It comes not only from that nothingness which, we are told, human reality strives to transcend only to fall back into it: It comes from the fear that this very refuge might be denied us, that there might not be nothing, that this nothing might belong still to the realm of being. From the moment that we can not escape from existence, then that existence is not completed, it can not be fully lived—and our struggle to live is a blind struggle which does not know that it struggles to die and which is ensnared in a possibility which becomes ever poorer. Our salvation is in death, but hope is life. It follows that we are never saved and yet never despairing; and it is in a certain sense our own hope that destroys us—it is hope that is the sign of our distress—so that distress also has a liberating value and leads us to hope ("Do not despair even of the fact that you do not despair. . . . Precisely that is called life.").

If each term, each image, each narrative is capable of signifying its contrary—and vice versa—then one must seek the cause in that transcendence of death which makes death attractive, unreal, and impossible, and which deprives us of the only absolute term, yet without depriving us of its mirage. It is death that masters us, but it masters us by its impossibility; and that means that we have not been born ("My life is the hesitation before birth"), but at the same time it means that we are absent from our death ("You ceaselessly talk of death and yet you do not die"). If the night, suddenly, is put into doubt, then there is no longer either day or night; there is no longer anything more than a vague, crepuscular light, which is sometimes memory of the day and sometimes regret for the night, end of the sun and sun of the end. Existence is interminable, it is no longer anything more than an indeterminacy; and we do not know whether we are excluded from this indeterminacy (and that is why we search in vain for a solid grip on it) or forever enclosed within it (and we turn in desperation towards the outside). This existence is an exile in the strongest meaning of the word: We are not there, we are elsewhere, and we will never cease to be there.

The theme of "The Metamorphosis" is an illustration of this torment of literature which has for its object its own lack and which draws the reader into a gyration where hope and distress answer one another without end. The condition of Gregor is precisely the condition of the being that cannot leave existence, for which to exist is to be condemned to falling always again into existence. Having become a vermin, he continues to live in the modality of the fall; he buries himself in animal solitude; he approaches as closely as is possible to the absurdity and impossibility of living. But what happens? Precisely this: He continues to live. He does not even try to escape his misfortune, but into the interior of this misfortune he transports a final resource, a final hope: He continues to fight for his place under the sofa, for his little trips over the freshness of the walls, for life itself amid filth and dust. And thus we, too, must hope along with him, since he hopes; but we must also despair of this frightening hope which pursues itself, without purpose, at the interior of the void. And then he dies: an intolerable death, in desolation and solitude—and yet an almost happy death because of the feeling of deliverance which it represents, because of the new hope for a finish which will be definitive in our time. But soon this last hope in its turn dissolves. It is not true, there has been no finish, existence continues; and the gesture of the young sister, her movement of awakening to life, of a call to sensual delight, with which the narrative ends, is the peak of horror—there is nothing more frightening in the whole story. It is the curse itself and it is also revival—it is hope—for the girl wants to live, and to live is already to escape the inevitable.

In all literature, the narratives of Kafka are among the blackest, among those most riveted to an absolute disaster. And they are also the ones that most tragically torture hope, not because hope is condemned, but because it does not succeed in being condemned. However complete the catastrophe may be, an infinitesimal margin subsists of which one does not know whether it preserves hope or, on the contrary, whether it banishes it forever. It is not enough that God himself submit to his own sentence and succumb with it in the most sordid collapse, in an unimaginable breakdown of scrap-metal and organs; one must still await his resurrection and the return of his incomprehensible justice which condemns us forever to terror and to consolation. It is not enough that the son, answering the unjustifiable and irrefutable verdict of his father, throw himself into the river with an expression of tranquil love for him; this death must be associated with the continuation of existence by the strange final phrase—"At this moment an unending stream of traffic ("circulation") was just going over the bridge"—whose symbolic value, whose precise physiological meaning, Kafka himself affirmed. And finally, and most tragically of all, Josef K. of *The Trial* dies, after a parody of justice, in the deserted suburb where two men execute him without a word. But it is not enough that he die "like a dog"; he must still have his part of survival: that of the shame which the infinity of a crime he did not commit reserves for him, by condemning him to live as well as to die.

"Death is in front of us almost like the painting of *The Battle of Alexander* on the wall of a classroom. From the moment of entering this life it is our task to obscure or even efface this painting by our acts." The works of Kafka are this painting which is death, and they are also the acts of obscuring and effacing it. But, like death, they have been unable to obscure themselves: On the contrary, they shine marvellously from the futile effort they have made to extinguish themselves. That is why we do not understand them except in the act of betraying them, and our reading turns anxiously in a circle around a misunderstanding.

Description of a Form

by Martin Walser

Description of a Complete Event in Kafka's Work

The event begins only at the moment when the disruption occurs. In *The Trial* this takes place before the beginning of the actual text, since it is not Josef K. but the court which is disrupted, having been attracted by Josef K.'s "guilt." However, since the narration is from the hero's viewpoint, the story begins only at the moment when the hero becomes aware of the ramifications of the disruption he has caused in the sensitive organism of the court. In *America* the event begins only at the moment when Karl learns of Schubal's unjust treatment of the stoker. In this moment, the world of illusory order is disrupted by Karl's purer sense of justice. Only in *The Castle* does the disruption coincide with the beginning of the work. These disruptions run counter to the traditional openings of epic structures. With Kafka there is no fictional display of the world into which the event is then fitted, no preparation; only *America* still retains traces of such preparation. When *The Trial* begins, the two antagonistic orders are already on the scene, the confrontation has already begun. The initial situation, which was inaugurated by the disruption, already implies the entire possible course of action until the end of the first event, which is marked by the first negation. But since the orders thereupon relapse automatically into their initial stance, the possibility is thus already present for another disruption and, consequently, for another negation. The disruption thus inaugurates the event by, as it were, awakening the counter-order, summoning it to the scene, and thereby bringing on the inevitable course of action. The K.s are responsible for the respective disruptions. They force the counter-world to concern itself with them. In its eyes that already makes them guilty. The "burden of proof" that the disruption is justified rests on the shoulders of the K.s. Our concept of "disruption" is, it goes without saying, framed in the perspective of the

---

From *Beschreibung einer Form: Franz Kafka*, by Martin Walser (Munich: Carl Hanser, 1961), pp. 92–3, 98–104, 116–127. Reprinted by permission of the author and of Carl Hanser Verlag. English version by the present editor; throughout, the problematic German word "aufheben" has been rendered as "negate."

counter-order to the K.s. However, the K.s cannot permit to be classified as disruption what for them is simply the assertion of their existence. That means that if they were to retract the disruption, as demanded by the counter-order, then they would have to negate their own existence; but it is precisely this they wish to assert, and so they disrupt. And this disruption is again negated by the counter-world in the manner already indicated; that it thereby negates the existence of the K.s happens to a certain extent unintentionally, as a by-product.

The negation is the caesura which concludes the event. That is the variable element in Kafka, the form of the void which, in the multiplicity of its fulfillment, brings the work into being.

The Rhythm of The Trial

The spacious rhythm in *America*, which is really only the rhythm of Karl's punishment, is no longer present in *The Trial*. The erection of mutually attuned orders whose confrontation is played out in a precisely functioning series of figural relationships—this basic situation no longer permits a long-breathed rhythm. Above all the rhythm is now no longer so one-sidedly confined to the negating caesura; Josef K.'s disruption is constituted not just by a question of principle, by a transcendent confrontation: Disruption has now been actualized as projecting in itself Joseph K.'s assertion of his existence.

The warders invade K.'s room, because guilt attracts the court. The disruption thus emanates from Josef K. If he wishes to defend himself, to declare his innocence, then the warders negate every defence, since he must admit that he does not know the law; how can he then claim innocence? To this is at once added a further negation by the Inspector, who makes all discussion impossible, since he is only a lowly official, whose only job is to communicate to K. the fact of his arrest. This first negation is thus achieved because K. is ignorant of the law, the second because the Inspector lacks access to these things. With this, everything is provisionally accomplished—from the court's viewpoint. It has responded to the disruption caused by K.'s "guilt." Now, however, K. himself begins to work (in the structural sense, one could say he begins to function). He has the feeling that he has caused a "great disorder" in "the whole household of Frau Grubach," and "that it was his task alone to put it right again." Indeed, he even believes that Frau Grubach would have to give him notice if she wanted to keep her house respectable. K. disrupts the order in the boarding-house. Thus there begins in this work a second series of events which interlocks with the one that is related directly to the court. The form of the void is valid for it, too. K. has disrupted life in the boarding-house; his efforts to calm it down again are subject to the rhythm of negation. The exchange with Frau Grubach and the compulsive replay of the interrogation in front of Fräulein Bürstner do not negate the disruption, do not restore the order; on the contrary, they negate K.'s efforts on behalf of order and make the disorder even greater. The third sequence of disruption and negation begins immediately thereafter in the bank: The negating force is the Assistant Manager. Then the action reverts to the realm of the court: K. invades the empty courtroom, supported by the usher's wife (disruption), she is carried away from him (negation); he recognizes this himself as his "first unequivocal defeat." His penetration of the offices (disruption) ends with a fainting spell; he is carried out (negation). After this, there is another incident in the boarding-house. In order to neutralize a disruption, he seeks an interview and is told: "Interviews are neither deliberately accepted nor refused." In the following chapter occurs the only passage which contains a positive reaction to an action of K.'s. But this reaction has the effect of making K. do all he can to undo it, to negate his own original action, because what he has wrought constitutes a disruption of the bank's order ("The Whipper").

Josef K. himself negates the efforts on his behalf of his uncle, for whom the trial is a painful disruption of the family's peace. The next negating force is the Lawyer. While K. is still thinking about the negation by the Lawyer, there follows immediately the entrance of the Assistant Manager to undermine his existence, his professional position (i.e. to negate it). After this there are the assertions of existence with Titorelli, again with the Lawyer and with the prison chaplain: All of them are subjected to negation.

That is the last of the attempts by Josef K. actually included in the work to assert himself, to end his trial. Since the court asserts that it is only attracted by guilt and is in fact attracted by Josef K., every attempt by K. to demonstrate his innocence, and thus to prevent the trial from properly getting under way, must constitute an act against the court, a disruption of its order. All the other accused submit; Josef K. disrupts—and therefore his efforts must be negated.

The trial is made up of three strands of action: the boarding-house, the bank, and the court. Here we can only give a suggestion of these strands; for, and this is precisely the advance in relation to *America*, the construction of this work is seamless—the three strands are intricately interwoven. Just as one effort follows another, so does one negation inevitably follow another. The boarding-house, the court, the bank—it really matters little where the sequence starts, the configuration is everywhere the same. The rhythm of these events is short-breathed, harsh, and decisive. There is no pause for rest, no digression, and no possibility of escape. The confrontation of the orders is not interrupted by long descriptions with K. as a mere spectator, as is the case with Karl in *America*; on the contrary, wherever K. may be, he is everywhere on trial. When he walks the street, there is laughter from the windows above him; when he sits in his office and thinks about his trial, the Assistant Manager enters laughing; when he comes home in the evening, he thinks he sees a guard in front of his house . . . ! His entire thinking is an uninterrupted effort to assert his existence; the events which intervene negate this effort completely automatically. Naturally all the turns for the better which helped to create the long-breathed rhythm in *America* are lacking here.

Because of this breathless rhythm of events, *The Trial* has repeatedly been labelled "dramatic" and indeed has been reworked for stage and radio. It would lead too far afield to compare the two versions with the original. Suffice it to say that of the original work there remain only feeble and somewhat distorted plot-summaries. Despite its apparently dramatic quality this work has resisted every dramatization. And why? Because the language is epic, and because with Kafka everything has being only through language. Because the variations on the form of the void, being basically repetitions, lack all dramatic impetus. Because in this prose there is no representation of an action that could be portrayed by actors. Activity is everything in this work, but the action is deprived of its effect-producing function. Insofar as it appears as action, it is a contribution to the debate in the form of a confrontation of orders. Action is no longer left in the sphere of mere behavior; rather, like everything else, it furthers a mode of thinking in terms of antagonistic orders. However, as soon as these events are torn out of the medium where alone they have poetic validity—the medium of language—and are rendered visible on stage through the medium of the human form—the actor—the confrontation of orders loses its real character. The total imaginative communication, which in the book is achieved through language, becomes on the stage an intricate visual perception which is already lacking in any effectiveness appropriate to Kafka because no actor can submit himself to the stylized gestural mechanics of the individual figures. The language itself degenerates into a dialogue operating through thesis and antithesis. The radio has indeed an advantage vis-à-vis the stage in that it can strive for a total imaginative communication and concentrate everything in it. However, as soon as the various figures achieve individuation, even if only through their "speaking," they are torn out of the epic network of the novel and lose their "clarity," because a human voice cannot "express" them in their functionality, which presupposes the novel's rhythmic movement. Reproduction on radio can doubtless lead further than is possible on the stage (although the versions hitherto have not managed it), but even radio has little prospect of doing full justice to the work. One is reminded of Döblin's remark about *Don Quixote*: "No one can rework the book *Don Quixote* into a drama, for the same thing happens in it a hundred times, in endlessly varied forms."

What seems to bring *The Trial* close to the dramatic is its closed quality;

it is the only one of the three "novels" that seems to have a "conclusion." So far we have disregarded this final chapter completely. Josef K. is executed; the variation of the events ceases. Kafka is not here constructing an ironic final chapter: He remains entirely within the world he has created—and yet we would insist that even this final chapter is not a genuine ending. To make the point by exaggeration: Had Kafka concretized the play of the conflicting orders in spools of thread (like Odradek) or in celluloid balls (as in the Blumfeld story), then the possibility of endless repetition would have received "objective" expression. As it is, however, he has juxtaposed with the nonfinite hierarchy of officialdom a human being who is, if we may phrase it thus, biologically finite. This person comes to an end, but the order he constitutes (qua being) cannot end. There is no necessity in *The Trial* requiring a cessation of the repetition of events. Josef K. simply ceases to continue his self-assertions, because he realizes that every assertion is necessarily followed by a negation. He has become tired of this game. He does not want to be without "common sense": "Are people to say of me after I am gone that at the beginning of my case I wanted to finish it, and at the end of it I wanted to begin it again?" he asks himself. He could thus prolong the trial. There is no insistence on an end emanating from the Court. On the contrary, he has been sent two "half-dumb, senseless creatures" and has "been left to say" to himself "all that is needed." He determines the path taken, the men obey him; he could summon the aid of a policeman, indeed the policeman seems to want to intervene of his own accord, "but K. forcibly pulled his companions forward." Shortly before the end K. is still reflecting: "Was help at hand? Were there arguments in his favor that had been overlooked? Logic is doubtless unshakable, but it cannot withstand a man who wants to go on living." The "logic" that the trial cannot be ended—that every assertion of existence is necessarily followed by negation—this logic is doubtless unshakable; but a man's will to live breaks through it insofar as he continues to live life despite this hopelessness and to assert his existence despite the unceasing negation. There are still "arguments," that is, assertions of existence he has not yet made; but K. no longer has the strength or the will to continue his self-assertions, therefore he gives himself up more or less voluntarily to the knife. This end is thus arbitrary, not necessary. Perhaps Kafka drew up this ending to satisfy a convention, since after all a novel must have an ending. Döblin says it is "purely accidental and externally imposed that Don Quixote happens to die." Properly understood, this applies to Kafka also. This "ending" thus does not contradict the "unlimited form" of this fiction. The only question is, how long a man can endure seeing his self-assertions incessantly negated. This "how long" is tied to the finitude of the individual person, but does not affect the infinite potentiality for reiteration inherent in the form of the void which prescribes that every self-assertion by one order is felt by the other as a disruption obliging it to negate the initial assertion. Don Quixote is also a mortal man, hence the possibility of Quixotic behaviour is in fact unlimited! This relationship of one existent being to another, of man thus constituted to his similarly constituted environment, this is the external rhythm which generates an infinite sequence of quite definite, predictable events. Thereby biological finitude is itself negated; it becomes a no longer fundamentally important substratum, since the reader is impelled towards the transcendental status of the orders as constituting the expressive basis of the work. This consideration may suffice to clarify, in *The Trial* as well as in *America*, a relationship between orders which is oriented toward infinity.

In *The Trial* three different series of events are interwoven. These circles function without interruption. A genuinely private circle, which would have given K. the possibility of rest such as is offered at intervals to Karl in *America* by the uncle and the cook, was in fact envisaged by Kafka, but not completed. And with good reason, or so it seems to us: The "journey to his mother" and the genuine friendship with the prosecuting counsel Hasterer would have weakened the inexorability of the trial. The equilibrium, which is from K.'s viewpoint a hopeless one, between assertion of existence and negation would have suffered. Mother and friend are foreign bodies in the circle of these automatically functioning figures. To maintain the work's intention, K. would have had to negate himself any efforts undertaken on his behalf by this "private" circle, just as he negates the efforts of the uncle. In the uncle's case this is still to some extent justified by Leni, because he wants to enlist her in his cause and neglects the uncle as a result; but here a fateful aspect of K. announces itself, namely that he always acts to his own detriment. According to the structure of the work, this aspect is only justified when he disrupts through his assertion and engenders a negation. If, however, he were to behave similarly with regard to his friend and his mother, the K.s' "ideal" relationship (in the sense of rhythmic articulation) to the officials would be discredited, because he would then have to deliver the proof himself that he acts even with regard to his closest helpers in such a way as to disrupt and be negated or to negate himself. That mother and friend could become real helpers is absolutely inconceivable; that would contradict the whole ground-plan of the work. There can be no real help for K.; he must assert his existence alone; whoever stands with him is either negated along with him (like the usher's wife) or else harms him (like Leni).

Kafka therefore limits himself to the three circles we have named—circles which he then displays in their common enterprise against K.

The Trial *as Epic Structure*

Kafka's world has totality. Totality is basic to the created world. In *America* one can still speak of a visible crystallization of totality: Karl and the counter-order develop only in the course of the book into orders constituting a total world. Both objectify themselves increasingly from one confrontation to the next. Since this world still has features of an empirical world, there are still dimensions there that are only hinted at, elements of being that do not enter fully into the work. In *The Trial* and *The Castle* Kafka no longer refers to an existing world. Through the articulation of his autonomous formal capacity he has overcome his subjectivity in advance of the creative act. What he now writes acquires, independently of him, objective being which, in its pure createdness, does not have to strive for a totality of empirical objects but which, in compensation, attains a totality of the forces that decide a human being's existence. Lukacs admits that even today a subjectivity which "is enthroned, far removed from life and dailiness, on the pure heights of being" could, in its structure, "incorporate all the essential conditions of totality and transform its own frontiers into those of the world." To be sure, Lukacs regards it as impossible that such a "separated" individual could produce epic literature. But that is precisely what Kafka has done. He is able to transform his own frontiers into those of his world. In this world, inwardness and action correspond in a manner paradigmatic for the true epic. The existence of the K.s and the actional infrastructure (self-assertion and negation) do not diverge; rather, they are harmonized through a masterly series of correspondences in order to achieve a judgment of man not in his "person" but in his "project" (which is here existence as such)—a judgment such as Hegel demands of the epic genre. The totality of functions which are significant for and against an existence is obvious at every moment and does not have to be gradually constructed. Therefore the "immanence of meaning" (Lukacs) is here not a problem that can only find its solution through a development within the work, as is usually the case in novels. Let us pursue this further: According to Lukacs an abstract system of ordering structural categories underlies the novel. The hero of the novel is the representative of this system. The reality which he confronts is hostile to the meaning of this system—the raison d'être of the hero—hence the hero is threatened by the counter-world. This abstract basis of the novel becomes form, argues Lukacs, when it perceives itself as abstract, that is, "the immanence of meaning demanded by form derives precisely from a ruthless insistence on uncovering its absence." This uncovering is a process, is none other than the "journey of the problematic individual to himself." The process implies qualitative changes, genuine developments.

Something emerges which could not be predicted at the outset. There was, then, certainly no totality present at the outset.

With Kafka, no journey of the hero to himself is necessary in order to bring the immanent meaning to the surface. Here the fact that the meaning is really meaningless is not uncovered only through a long struggle of the hero against his environment; rather, the meaning is expressly present in the very first action. Qualitatively, nothing can be changed, either in the world of the orders, which appears from the start as a totality, or in any of its representatives. This created world exists in the repetition, not the development, of its parts.

The relationship of the parts to the whole is an essential criterion for the classification of a work as a novel or as an epic. Aristotle was of the opinion that the "form must be closed in such a way that, were one to move or remove a single part, the whole would collapse or at least be shaken." The action, he said, must have a beginning, middle, and end. All this we would ascribe to the novel. Hegel, who lends the greatest importance to this problem, demands that a "basic mood, explicated and illustrated" in the various parts, declare itself as the "all-pervading unity, holding together and enfolding into itself the totality of the specifics." For Hegel there must be no teleological relationship between the parts and the whole, because otherwise the parts would be reduced to their functionality and there would result, not an "organic totality," but a "prosaic purposefulness." Lukacs demands of the epic an "organic, homogeneous consistency," and of the novel a "contingent, heterogeneous discreteness."

In Kafka the parts are never heterogeneous, since they are exclusively variations of a single form of the void. Even the seemingly episodic sections of the Barnabas story or the analyses of the doorkeeper fable are variations of this kind. They never have to justify their presence in the work through serving some kind of compositional purpose; they do not have to transcend their "simple being" because they are homogeneous with the whole and merge with it organically through the fact that they constitute it. How little these parts, in the later works, owe to a compositional purpose is clear from the many incomplete chapters left by Kafka, the absence of which in no way detracts from the work. This is also underlined by the fact that doubts can be raised about the order of the chapters in *The Trial*, the work that has been called the most self-contained. Charles Neider insists that the correct sequence of the early chapters is: one, four, two, five, three. Since Neider's arguments derive from considerations based on content, with a view to giving the events the shape of a clearer "plot," we will not pursue them further. Neider's chapter sequence is doubtless as well justified as the one arranged by Brod. Very dubious, however, like all psychoanalytical experiments inflicted on Kafka, is Neider's argument that the fifth chapter must precede the third because Josef K., in his actions towards the accused men in the attic, is clearly under the influence of the whipper's sadism.

That one can discuss the chapter arrangement in this way is probably sufficient proof of the self-sufficiency of the parts. These parts intensify the theme through variation of it; they produce no development, but give a dynamism to the whole through their perpetual motion within themselves. We have shown how assertion and negation function as the engine of this motion, which is both initiated and concluded within itself.

"The truly epic principle of composition is simple addition," says Emil Staiger. The intensifying repetition, through variation, of the form of the void is, in compositional terms, nothing but addition. With Kafka, to be sure, thanks to his basic rhythm of solipsistic reduction, the addition is the precise opposite of that of the original epic from which Staiger gains his concept. The condition of Homer's parataxis is the spontaneous interest he brings to each and every object. The exhaustive description of things leads to what Goethe and Schiller called "retardation"; the opposite stylistic mode is called by Auerbach "suspense."

If we are to demonstrate that Kafka stands closer to the epic than to the novel, these stylistic modes must be discussed in relation to Kafka. We begin the discussion with a comparison of certain expressive elements in Homer and in Kafka. Homer's rationalism is constantly praised: "Homer's brightness is enlightenment" (Staiger)—the point is stressed by Auerbach also. We are concerned, however, not so much with the source of Homer's "brightness" as with the expressive elements engendered by it in the work itself: The tangible immediacy of all phenomena distinguishes all areas of this work; indeed the brightness increases in the "realm of the shining divinities," in "Zeus' kingdom of light."

We have seen that precisely the opposite is the case with Kafka: Here the exclusive focus on K.'s reactions is brought about by darkness. A stereotypical mode of interpretation becomes the expression of his being, especially in relation to the hierarchies which, in contrast to Homer, become ever more unclear the more exalted they are. This endless interpreting, in which all the characters also participate in principle, since the darkness is general, engenders the retardation in Kafka's works. This results, then, from a phenomenon precisely antithetical to Homer: There brightness compels detailed description, here darkness compels endless interpretation. Homer's work is full of objects, Kafka's almost empty.

Now the word "retardation" immediately places the phenomenon of which we speak in opposition to teleological development (Goethe and Schiller develop this meaning for the word and generally use it thus). There is, in the genuine epic form, no retardation in the real meaning of the word. Pausing, dwelling on each moment, is not retardation since there is nothing to hold back. For Homer and Kafka there is no goal; or, rather, there is no way to the goal, because the goal is already attained in every instant. Dwelling on the object is as automatic for Homer, as free of ulterior motive structurally, as the endlessly circling interpretations of Kafka's characters. In both cases there is no pausing on the way; rather, there is always a state of already having arrived at the goal. This eternal circling around the same point prevents, in Kafka, the emergence of any suspense, any "curiosity concerning the subject matter" (Beissner), and is the necessary complement to the reiterated variation of the form of the void. As with Homer, where the individual hexameter mirrors the self-contained objectivity of the world, so Kafka's sentence structure in its differentiation is the basic element that mirrors the work as a whole.

Let us try to show, through an example from the work itself, how little value Kafka places on "development" in his work. We choose a section from *The Trial*, to which particularly dramatic qualities have been ascribed. First of all, this section (the beginning of Chapter Seven) is largely presented in indirect speech, and for that reason is already deprived of all activity. Josef K. is thinking about his relationship to the lawyer. In a real trial, what is here expressed in ten pages would have to be said in two or three sentences: The lawyer has made the plea, but nothing definite can be said about the success of such a plea because not enough is known about the nature of the legal authority. The principle of negation could easily be given concrete form through such compression. But such a teleological thrust is foreign to Kafka.

He begins with the initial statement:

1. The lawyer has prepared the first plea. It is very important. . . . There follows, necessarily:
1A. Unfortunately it probably will not be read at the Court, because. . . . Thereby Kafka can, without having moved forward in the slightest, add on a second statement:
2. When all the materials are collected, all the pleas are read.

But:

2A. Unfortunately that usually doesn't happen, because they are misplaced or lost.
2Aa. Even if they are not lost, they are hardly read at all.

Now begins a bridge-passage to two larger series. The lawyer states that the situation is regrettable but justified, *because:* This "because" inaugurates a series of additions which chiefly contain negations of K. However, small counter-negations (generated by the lawyer himself) are incorporated into the series, designed to prevent the extinction of all hope and to prepare a new counter-negation which will annul the whole movement of negation. First, then, the negating series. It begins with a completely neutral sentence: The proceedings may be public, but do not have to be; from this, the following inferences are drawn:

3Aa. The indictment is inaccessible.
b. One therefore doesn't know on what the plea should be focused.
c. The particulars of the indictment can only be guessed at.
d. The defence is in a difficult situation.
e. That is intentional, since a defence is not permitted.
f. It is only tolerated. Even that is uncertain.
g. Hence there are only petty lawyers (proofs follow).
h. The attempt is even made to shut out the defence as far as possible. In this series of utterances the aim appears to have been a progressive clarification of the situation. However, now commences the negation of these negations of K. (a negation of the negation of his existence, hence a new series of possibilities).

3Ba. "Nothing could be more mistaken" than to regard the lawyers as unnecessary.
b. On the contrary; with no court are they as important as with this one. Now follows:
c. A new series of proofs of the lawyer's importance, which branches out again in its turn. This series concludes that personal connections with the court are the most important thing.

From this derives the occasion for a new important statement:

4. K.'s choice is very fortunate, since Dr. Huld enjoys the most favorable connections.
4A. To be sure, one must not hope for too much from this, because. . . .

Nevertheless, a new statement becomes possible:

5. The judges are dependent on the defence, because. . . .
5A. There now follow four negating series:
a. Organization of the court.
b. Treatment of the lawyers.
c. Attitude of the accused.
d. Experiences of the way trials turn out.

And only now does the conversation return to the "first plea." After a further series of negations the conversation ends without result, as we indicated earlier.

The theme of the work has become transparent from a multiplicity of facets, yet within the work nothing has progressed. A part of the whole has come into being; it has become a part through the parataxis of even smaller parts and can now be joined to the other parts through the process of epic addition. It is obviously impossible to indicate schematically the uncommonly subtle web of motifs of which such a part is composed. Our purpose was merely to show that there is no retardation here, since even the smallest part always justifies in and for itself its presence in the work. Suspense is out of the question, because the smallest initiative toward a development is immediately smothered by a negation. This leads to a certain monotony, even to boredom. This element is indubitably present in Kafka's work; it is an element to be found in every genuine epic.

This example serves also to demonstrate once again that assertion, negation, and then modification of the latter are realized in the very movement of the individual sentence. Only by virtue of the fact that Kafka's prose is able to consummate the turn from assertion to negation in a single sentence can the individual sentence prevent all development and engender a new parataxis. We cannot here adequately characterize this prose; yet one particular feature should be stressed that makes it a genuine epic prose: We mean the tendency towards the formulaic. Homer's formulae for heroes and gods are well known. With Kafka, of course, we do not find completely identical recurring images. We already pointed out the recurring figures whose similarity could be traced to a structural mechanism that encloses the individual figure and is defined by function. None of these figures is endowed with an individual language. The formulaic quality of this language becomes clearest in the comments on the hierarchies: The adjectives "small" and "large," "low" and "high," are deployed against each other in an exaggeratedly contrasting manner in order to express both the greatness of the authorities themselves and the gulf between them and the K.s. In *The Castle*, K. is designated quite simply as "the lowest" and Klamm as "the highest." When Huld explains his connections with the higher judges they are only "higher officials of subordinate rank, naturally"; at another point the "highest examination of the lowest school" is taken. The examining magistrate with whom Josef K. can still deal is "the lowest of the low examining magistrates"; Josef K.'s warders also know only the "lowest ranks" of the officials; the doorkeeper asserts that he is powerful, although he is only the "lowest doorkeeper" and although the sight of the third man above him is already more than he can stand. How complicated this official activity is is also expressed in simple formulae: In *The Castle* even the "hardest worker" cannot keep together all the ramifications of "even the smallest occurrence on his desk."

These contrasted superlatives, present in multiple variations throughout Kafka's work, strike every reader of Kafka. They contribute above all to conveying the presence of the orders as entities, to portraying their "selfness" (Staiger) despite all the blurring of their outline.

After this discussion of "retardation," its origin and its mode of functioning, which was designed to clarify the self-sufficiency of the parts in Kafka's work, we will now proceed to investigate the functional role of time and space in this fiction.

The space in which the confrontation of the orders takes place is not empirical. It is, in its essence, created; it has a function. Through the exclusive focus on the hero's impressions, and through all the other data concerning spatial organization, it becomes clear that space is present solely as an expressive element and as such serves a constructive purpose. Thus it is one of the hierarchy's essential modes of functioning. The orders are characterized by their spatial position. This space is not constant: Qualitatively different spatial entities are possible. The offices of the court, Huld's room, Titorelli's attic, the landlady's annex, the mayor's room, the bar, the secretary's room: These are not merely scenery to be changed in order to make the action more lively; they are, rather, levels of the hierarchy and, as such, negating forces when the K.s bring their self-assertions into their domain. How inconstant this space is, how much its character is subordinated to its function of the moment, is shown by the expressive effect Kafka achieves when he "violates" the natural spatial contours: The journey of the country doctor, traversed once at lightning speed and then with interminable slowness, is emblematic of this. When K. starts out towards the castle, his path, while not leading him away from the castle, also brings him no closer, because between K. and the castle there lies a space that can never be crossed by K. Frieda's suggestion that they emigrate to southern France or Spain is an ironic Utopia that cannot refer to any geographical relation.

Kafka proceeds similarly in his treatment of time: As a duration, as a conditioning factor for the action, it is negated. Since the individual parts have no teleological link to the whole, since they serve no compositional function like the postulation of a beginning, a middle, and an end, time, which necessarily implies progression and development, cannot as such play a role in the work. Kafka uses it merely as an expressive tool.

Concerning the seasons, Pepi tells us in *The Castle*: "Winter has been with us long, a very long winter, and monotonous. . . . Well, yes, some day spring comes too, and summer, and there's a time for that too, I suppose; but in memory, now, spring and summer seem as short as though they didn't last much longer than two days, and even on those days, even during the most beautiful day, even then sometimes snow falls." But when Kafka wants to portray the humiliated Barnabas family after their condemnation, he has them sit in a room "with the windows shut in the heat of July and August." In this village it is dark an hour or two after breakfast. Kafka is unconcerned with the "natural" sequence of time. He has K. state on the second day of his stay in the village that he is now in his fourth day there. (To be sure we have to calculate carefully in order to establish that it is only the second day; the narrator does not desert the hero's perspective to tell us something so unimportant.) Time has no conditioning effect; when it "seems" to Hans Castorp as though he has been, not one day, but "already a long time" on the Magic Mountain, then he is making a necessary connection with the effect of this "long time"; he feels he has "become older and wiser" during his stay.

It is just this kind of development that is impossible for K., as indeed development of any kind is impossible. Kafka deploys temporal elements solely in order to contrast them with the natural flow of time and thereby to achieve expressive effect. When Josef K. opens the door of the lumber-room the day after he has witnessed the whipping, he finds "everything still the same, exactly as he had found it . . . the previous evening . . . the whipper with his rod and the warders with all their clothes off . . . ."

Kafka's stories occur outside temporal laws. Since the meaning of the whole is immanent in every moment of the narration, there can be no overarching temporal context. "The decisive moment in human development is always present": thus did Kafka formulate the implications of this for his own existence.

In conclusion, let us summarize the principal features which place Kafka's fictions in the proximity of genuine epics:

1. The articulation of an autonomous formal capacity assures the *objectivity* of these fictions.

2. The pure createdness of his world frees Kafka from the requirement, which can only be fulfilled to a limited extent in any case, of creating an empirical totality as a representation; his world *has totality*.

3. In this totality, which is present from the start, development is impossible; hence *the parts are self-contained* and linked into a whole through parataxis alone.

4. The theme of this epic structure is the confrontation of two orders; the confrontation is articulated through the varied *repetition of an event* (form of the void); it is conceived as literally interminable.

5. The syntax and vocabulary, with their tendency toward the *formulaic*, constitute a genuine epic language.

It is probably unnecessary to insist that these notes in no way add up to the assertion that Kafka created epics in the Homeric sense. Georg Lukacs, Emil Staiger, and Friedrich Schmidt have long placed such attempts at restoration in the correct perspective and have demonstrated the unrepeatability of the original form. Our argument is designed above all to illustrate the gulf that separates Kafka's fictions from what is usually called the novel. If one could agree to apply the concept "epic" not only to the works of a specific stage in the development of individual cultures, if, further, one could free this concept from its false application to pastoral novels and family chronicles, then, in my opinion, it could be used again today as a valid genre concept. Kafka's fictions prompt such a usage. Like Cervantes' *Don Quixote*, indeed more so, they elude the categories of the novel.

The Role of Women

by Wilhelm Emrich

Three women come Josef K.'s way: Miss Bürstner, the wife of the court usher, and Leni. They represent three possible attitudes of woman as she relates to the court: (1) standing outside the court, (2) living in conflict with it, and (3) succumbing completely to its power.

Miss Bürstner is the free, independent woman. She is therefore of paramount importance to the whole of Josef K.'s trial.

She has little "experience in legal matters," but she "would like to know everything, and legal matters, particularly, interest me very much. A court of justice has a peculiar attraction, don't you think?" (P 37–38). But precisely in relation to her, Josef K. fails. Properly speaking, *he* would have to take her to court. But "what it is all about," in this matter of his prosecution at court, he himself "does not know." Miss Bürstner is "inordinately disappointed" about this (P 38). Since Josef K. does not move freely toward his self, toward his own court of justice, it is not possible for a genuine love encounter to take place with another free self, one who would like to "know everything" about the "peculiarly" attractive court. As long as Josef K. flees from himself, there exists no bridge between him and someone with whom he could be on intimate terms; and the two cannot open their hearts to one another, mutual "knowledge" cannot be passed on from one to the other, love cannot spring into being. This unmarried Miss Bürstner, on the threshold of the secret of life and love, full of expectation but still lacking in "experience," could attain to a genuine encounter with Josef K. only if he were himself already a person in the full sense of the word; that is, if he were already in and at the same time *above* the court, and did not remain entangled in the mysterious powers of life. He succumbs to these unknown and uncontrollable powers instead of defeating them decisively.

In relation to the girl, Josef K. becomes a "thirsty animal" that avidly

---

From *Franz Kafka: A Critical Study of His Writings*, by Wilhelm Emrich, translated by Sheema Zeben Buehne, pp. 337–341. Copyright © 1968 by Frederick Ungar Publishing Co., Inc. Reprinted by permission of the publisher. Abbreviations refer to standard German texts: P = *Der Prozess*; H = *Hochzeitsvorbereitungen auf dem Lande*; T = *Tagebücher*.

seeks "water at the spring." With that, he has pronounced his own death sentence. "Finally he kissed her on the neck, low on her throat, and here he let his lips linger long" (P 42). His kiss is a deadly threat to his partner; it is the catastrophe of love, and it prefigures the scene of his destruction, that scene with his murderers, in which "hands . . . were placed on K.'s throat" (P 272).

Josef K. knows this himself. When he catches sight of "Miss Bürstner" on the night of his execution, he becomes "aware of . . . the uselessness of his resistance." He intended "not to forget the admonition that she [Miss Bürstner] signified for him" (P 268). This admonition is to the effect that "it has been left up to me to tell myself what is needed" (P 269); that is, to execute sentence upon himself, to commit suicide. "K. now knew with certainty that it would have been his duty . . . to take hold of the knife himself and bury it in himself" (P 271). But even for that he does not have the strength. He has to be executed by theater supernumeraries and puppets, together with whom he constitutes "only something lifeless." Where a spiritual free love encounter is denied, only rigid lifelessness can prevail.

However, this positive "admonition," signified for him by Miss Bürstner, has yet another meaning. After their first nocturnal encounter Miss Bürstner had definitely turned away from and consistently blocked Josef K.'s every attempt to resume contact with her, no matter if it was only an attempt to talk things over with her. In this way she referred him to himself. And this very denying him any help was the true and only help. This was the "admonition" that he "did not forget" and that, even on his way to execution, shows him where his help lies: in his decision "to tell myself what is needed."

In contrast with Miss Bürstner, who is unmarried, the usher's wife is in the very midst of matters of the court. When she directs Josef K., as he goes to the courtroom for the first time, she appears as "a young woman with gleaming black eyes, who happened to be washing baby clothes in a tub" (P 51). But she lives in conflict with the court. "It is really so disgusting here," she says (P 66). She has to give herself to the student attached to the court and to the examining judge, if her husband is not to lose his "position" (P 65). For the court is "powerful." She hopes she will be liberated through Josef K. "If you'll take me along, I'll go wherever you wish . . . I'll be happy to be away from here for as long a time as possible—best of all, forever" (P 72). From Josef K. she expects an "improvement" of the entire judicial system (P 66). And even her own husband believes that "only a man like" Josef K. could destroy the student's "power," could dare to give him a thrashing and wrest his wife away from him. And his reason for believing this is that Josef K. is "being prosecuted" (P 79). Only the defendants are free in relation to the court and not within the sway of this judicial organization.

Naturally Josef K. is unable to understand this. For in his opinion it would be particularly the defendants who would have to fear most from the power of the court, since the outcome of each trial depended on the court. " 'Yes, of course,' said the court usher, as if K.'s point of view were just as correct as his own" (P 79).

Here again is an instance where two mutually exclusive points of view appear as truth. And even the court usher's wife exists in a state of self-contradiction. While the student, at the order of the examining judge, is dragging her away, Josef K. cries out, " 'And you don't want to be set free?' . . . 'No,' cried the woman and warded K. off with both hands, 'no, no, not that at all, above all, not that! What can you be thinking of! That would be the ruin of me' " (P 74–75).

However, Josef K. clearly feels that he should nevertheless have set her free. He is "raging with disappointment . . . he realized that this was the first indubitable defeat that he had suffered at the hands of these people" (P 75). The antinomy is of course unresolvable. The liberation of the woman would actually be her ruin. But, by not daring to set her free, he comes all the more profoundly into the power of the court instead of receiving the anticipated "help." Deliverance, in the opinion of the court usher, is possible only in one's ". . . dream . . . I wouldn't know of any . . . other help" (P 78). Reconciliation is a "dream," dreamed in a "night darker than has ever yet existed." Reconciliation takes for granted the renunciation of any kind of help, the hazard of "ruin," the courage to be moved by a love that is no longer "within this world."

The third attitude is represented by Leni, who identifies completely with the judicial system and who urges Josef K. "not to be so unyielding—one cannot really defend oneself against this court; one has to make a confession" (P 132). She does not want to be liberated; on the contrary, she wants to make every defendant subject to her and to the court. Josef K. is "pulled down" by her. " 'Now you belong to me,' she said" (P 135). There "issued from her a bitter, provocative odor, like that of pepper." Her hand, of which she is "proud," gives the impression of a "pretty claw," because the connecting web of skin between her third and fourth fingers extends almost to the uppermost joint of her short fingers (P 134–35).

Claw and web—these are the aids afforded by a total engagement with life. To swim with the current, to drag down to her with her claws anyone who is unyielding—that is her recipe for life. For there can be no doubt that this is what lies behind the image of the web. Repeatedly in his works Kafka has developed the antinomy between swimming and nonswimming. Those who, like Hunter Gracchus, have stepped out of the stream of life, Kafka designates as "erstwhile swimmers" (T 22). And the truly "great swimmers" are for him the "nonswimmers" as well (H 319 ff.). Leni, however, is one who is unhesitatingly swimming in the stream of life.

Her kisses are at the same time bites. Her "love," so far as she is concerned, is an "exchange." She wants to be exchanged for Elsa, Josef K.'s mistress, but of course only when she learns from him that Elsa could never sacrifice herself for him. The ancient fairy-tale motif of being freed by a loving, self-sacrificing maiden from an evil enchantment and imprisonment crops up here, but the motif is in reverse. No hope of deliverance is possible for a defendant who is seeking aid from the outside. This acts as an incentive to her to carry off the hopeless man as booty. For Leni does not think in terms of sacrifice. Her "kiss, undirected, landed on his back as he was leaving" (P 135). She brings under her sway only the defendants; these, one and all without exception, she finds "handsome" for the very reason that they are outsiders, branded with the mark of Cain—this is what makes the lost ones extremely attractive; this is what promises exceptional pleasure in domineering them. Moreover, she long ago became expert at the entire erotic play with these "handsome" devotees, having had excellent practice with Huld the lawyer, to whom, for his "entertainment," she relates her conquests. When Block the businessman is forced to humiliate and exhibit himself masochistically in the presence of the two of them, "K. felt as if he were hearing a rehearsed conversation that had already been often repeated, that would yet be often repeated" (P 232). She plays a part in the monotonous world comedy of this court; she has "a doll-like, rounded face" (P 122).

Not until he is in the presence of such enslavement, however, is Josef K. able to gain the insight that now, finally, he must conduct the trial himself, renounce outside help, and give notice to the lawyer as well as to the latter's strange "nurse"—must shake them both off. . . .

The Legend of the Doorkeeper and Its Significance for Kafka's Trial

by Ingeborg Henel

The question has repeatedly been raised whether we are dealing, in Kafka's works, with allegories, with symbols, or with a special kind of myth. This question is important, for the answer we give conditions the answer to the other fundamental question: What kind of reality does Kafka portray in his works? Does he show us an inner reality by means of the image of an external world? Does he, with the help of allegories, point towards a conceptual system? Does he give us models of relationships which can be filled out with sociological, psychological, or metaphysical materials? Or is his fictional world a symbol of a transcendental world, whether this be of a positive or a negative character? If one of these questions is answered decisively in the affirmative, the interpretation becomes, in general, dogmatic and contradictory. But an outright negative answer to these questions is also unsatisfying, for Kafka is far less a realist, a surrealist, or a purveyor of mere absurdities than he is an allegorist or a symbolist. Now Kafka did in fact occasionally make use of an unambiguous traditional form, namely the parable. On the basis of his short parables, which at least stylistically present no puzzles, it should thus be easier to gain an understanding of the images that constitute Kafka's world. His most important parable is that of the doorkeeper, the only section from *The Trial* which he published in his lifetime. In his diary Kafka admits to having experienced "feelings of joy and satisfaction" upon rereading the legend of the doorkeeper. We can therefore assume that in this brief parable he succeeded in giving genuine expression to an essential concern, for he was his own severest critic. Although the legend, divorced from the context of the novel and presented on its own, as in the volume *A Country Doctor*, is exceedingly hard to understand, nevertheless its meaning should initially be sought, as far as possible, in an immanent reading of the text itself.

From *Deutsche Vierteljahrsschrift für Literaturwissenschaft und Geistesgeschichte*, vol. 37 (1963), pp. 50–70. Reprinted by permission of the author. The English version is by the editor of the present volume.

The Legend of the Doorkeeper

A man from the country comes to the ever open door of the law and wants to enter, but a doorkeeper forbids him to do so. All pleas and attempts at bribery are useless, and the man spends the rest of his life waiting in front of the open door. Shortly before his death he asks the doorkeeper why no one else has ever sought admittance to the law and is informed that this door had been intended for him alone.

How is it to be explained that the man is prevented from entering the door designed specifically for him? That the entrance is intended only for him must signify that he should have made use of it. It is thus a question of an omission on the part of the man, who has spent his life waiting in vain before the open door intended for him. A diary entry of December 4, 1913, written within the year in which the legend was conceived, confirms this hypothesis: "To see folly in every emotion that strives straight ahead and makes one forget everything else. What, then, is non-folly? Non-folly is to stand like a beggar before the threshold, to one side of the entrance, to rot and collapse" (*Diaries I*, p. 317). The word "fool" is used here in the way St. Paul uses it: "If any man among you seemeth to be wise in this world, let him become a fool, that he may be wise" (*I Corinthians*, 3, 18). For non-folly one could substitute, in St. Paul's sense, the term worldly wisdom or false wisdom. Worldly wisdom, obedience to the external law, prevents entry into the true law. The man from the country, as he squats on the stool outside the door to his goal and begs the fleas in the doorkeeper's fur coat for assistance, has taken the form of a beggar whose life is no life but a gradual process of decay. Fear of the first doorkeeper, who is not even terrifying and powerful like the other doorkeepers, has literally mesmerized him at the spot by the entrance; it has degraded and humiliated him (as the tradesman Block is humiliated), and in the end it makes him childish. The legend does not explain why the doorkeeper forbids the man entrance, but it makes it abundantly clear that the man, by submitting to the prohibition, gives up his humanity and misses the meaning of his life.

When we speak of parables we think in the first instance of Biblical parables, and the parable "Before the Law" is indeed related to these. Like the Biblical parables, it serves the purpose of making comprehensible to the listener his own situation and his own duty, by presenting both to him through an analogous case which, however, does not affect him directly. In this way impartial judgment is to be preserved, and thereby ultimate application to the listener's own case is to be made possible. Kafka indicates expressly his legend's relationship to the Bible by having the priest who narrates it speak of "scripture," of its "unalterability" and its "interpretations." As in the Bible, Kafka has the exposition follow the parable. But his explanations do not have the same status as Jesus' interpretations of his parables: They are mere learned exegeses, and thus lacking in authority, ambiguous, and even contradictory. Hence they must be understood, not as absolutely valid statements, but rather as experimental attempts to lead the listener, through assertion and counter-assertion, to an independent judgment.

If a parable is supposed to explain a given situation, then it is also in its turn explained through its relationship to this situation. So it is with the legend of the doorkeeper. The priest tells it in order to enlighten Josef K. concerning his situation and his mistakes, but one must be familiar with this situation in order fully to grasp the intent of the priest and the meaning of his story. Thus before we can continue with the interpretation of the legend and investigate its connection with Josef K., we must focus on his state of mind at the time of his visit to the cathedral.

Several months, perhaps half a year, have passed since Josef K.'s arrest, and he has learned to perceive that his trial is not going well. But the thought has not occurred to him that he is perhaps not conducting his trial in the correct manner. At his arrest he ignored the inspector's admonition that he occupy himself less with his innocence and the authorities and reflect more about himself; and since then he has done nothing but insist on his innocence and alternately accuse the authorities and plead for their help. Now the priest confronts him and repeats the admonition of the inspector. There are clear parallels between the arrest and the conversation with the priest. On both occasions Josef K. is addressed by a higher authority—and for the same purpose. On both occasions a kind of solemnity prevails: At the arrest this consists in the merely external trappings of the black suit; in the cathedral, on the other hand, it derives from the sacredness of the place. On both occasions Josef K. is summoned by a cry, which frightens him because it seems to come from another dimension. The first time it is a peremptory military cry, the second time a powerful call from the pulpit. At the arrest as in the cathedral, Josef K. thinks of flight. If he then remains after all this happens, it is not because he has summoned his courage, but because he cannot resist the power of the call. As at his arrest, Josef K. insists on his innocence to the priest also. And just as the inspector admonishes K. not to make such a fuss about his feeling of innocence, so the priest replies to K.'s assertion that he is a man like any other and innocent: "That's how all guilty men talk." At his arrest Josef K. does not, amazingly, ask what he is accused of—merely by whom—and inquires as to what authority the warders and the inspector represent. At the meeting with the priest, Josef K.'s interest is still directed at the authorities and the judges. In their weaknesses he sees both the source of his entanglement in a trial and his chance of influencing the trial favorably. At his first interrogation he adopted the pose of a judge condemning the court's practices. Now he responds to the priest's question as to what he intends to do about his trial with an assertion of hope that he can exploit the court's corruption to his own advantage. Even now he is still assigning guilt to others and seeking help from others; and just as he failed to heed the inspector's advice, so now he pays no attention to the priest's warning cry. He notices, to be sure, that the priest means well by him, but he does not understand that he is trying to pull him back from the abyss. From him, too, he is hoping for help, without grasping that the priest has already given him the only genuine help, namely the advice not to rely on outside help. Therefore the priest reaches for one last tool for curing Josef K. of his blindness: He tells him the legend of the doorkeeper.

Kafka's text is at this point completely unambiguous. When Josef K. explains to the priest that he is an exception among all who belong to the court, and that he has more confidence in him than in the others, the priest gives the surprising reply: "Don't be deluded." And when K. asks, uncomprehendingly, "How am I being deluded?" the priest responds, "You are deluding yourself about the Court"; and then proceeds directly to the legend with the words "In the writing which preface the law that particular delusion is described thus. . . ." The purpose of the legend is thus to show Josef K. his error concerning the court and its representatives. This error consists first in his belief that he can win his case through the help of the authorities, if only he influences them correctly; and second in his shifting responsibility for the bad state of his trial onto the officials of the court, who, since he gets no help from them, seem to him incompetent and evil. In the parable the first error is symbolized in the pleading and attempts at bribery of the man from the country; the second, more dangerous, error in the fact that the man does not accept responsibility for his actions. He willingly gives himself up to his delusion concerning the power of the doorkeeper, and regards the latter's prohibition as an absolute obstacle to entry into the law. His wretched degeneration outside the entrance is the verdict on his delusion.

Josef K. understands immediately the analogy between himself and the man from the country on the one hand, and the court and the doorkeeper on the other hand, and reacts to the story by identifying himself completely with the man from the country and defending him passionately. He fends off any reproach against the man from the country, and hence himself, by charging the doorkeeper with deception and portraying the man from the country as the victim of his deception. The discussion which follows between the priest and Josef K. concerning the doorkeeper —whether he is a deceiver or is himself deceived; whether, as an employee of the law, he is responsible also to the man from the country or only to the law—revolves basically around the question of where the responsibility lies for the man's wasted life and for Josef K.'s bungled trial. Josef K. wants to shift all guilt from the man to the doorkeeper (hence from himself to the court officials). Against this view the priest argues that the doorkeeper as an official is not free and is responsible only to the law, not to the man from the country, whereas the man, being free, bears the full responsibility for his actions.

To understand this argument one must know what being an official means for Kafka. In his concluding observation the priest says of the doorkeeper that everything he says is *necessary*. In this the doorkeeper stands in contrast to the man from the country and to Josef K., who are both free. The doorkeeper, insofar as he is an official, is unfree, impersonal, and subject to a necessity which neither he himself nor the others understand. Like an inanimate object, he cannot be reached or influenced by any human appeal. As becomes still clearer in *The Castle*, there can be no human contact with officials; one cannot even approach them externally, glimpse their faces. The questions which the doorkeeper addresses to the man from the country are "impersonal"; he accepts, to be sure, the man's gifts, but does not allow himself to be bribed, that is, influenced by them. Officials have no responsibility towards other people; their justification lies solely in their function—their calling—with which they are completely identical. This mere facticity and functionality of the officials must be accepted like the facticity of the material world. It detaches the officials from the sphere of human judgment by classifying them with the world of objects, in which there is no guilt and no responsibility. With this classification, however, the officials receive at the same time a certain dignity—not the dignity of a free, autonomous human being, but the externally conferred dignity of their necessary status, their office. It is manifest in their appearance, in the stiffness of their facial expressions (the doorkeeper's pointed nose and Tartar beard), and in their clothing (the black uniform of the warders with the useful-looking pockets).

On the one hand, the office gives the official dignity, support, and security, it relieves them, together with their freedom, of the burden of responsibility and guilt and thus renders them unassailable; but, on the other hand, the human element in them suffers and yearns for liberation, as the official Bürgel in *The Castle* admits to the landsurveyor. The officials secretly long to be released from their official state, yet they are simultaneously afraid of this possibility. The usher's wife involves herself with K. because she sees the possibility of liberation through him, and yet she thinks such a liberation would be the ruin of her. Officials cannot exist in freedom, they live merely through their calling, their function; that is why they work uninterruptedly and, moreover, in unventilated rooms, for fresh air, like anything free, is intolerable to them. But none is so exclusively an official that he does not at least have minor human weaknesses. In the doorkeeper, too, such traits emerge: patience and sympathy, naivete and presumption, which are labeled by the priest as "breaches in the character of the doorkeeper."

Seen from the outside, as objects, everyone appears as an official. Titorelli explains to Josef K. that all people, even the young girls, belong to the court; hence all are officials, and even he himself, the artist, is not really an exception. The participants at the first interrogation, whom Josef

K. at first believes to be members of two different parties, the prosecution and the defense, belong in fact to a single party: All wear the same badges, all belong as prosecutors to the court, hence all are officials and stand, like the doorkeeper in relation to the man from the country, as obstacles in Josef K.'s path, in the literal as well as the metaphorical sense.

Both Josef K. and the landsurveyor deal only with officials and their hangers-on. That means that they themselves are the only personalities in the novel; all the other figures confront them as objects, as part of the world. Gerhard Kaiser notes that *The Trial* is written from the hero's viewpoint, and that the world appears in it only as an object to the hero. Included in this world-as-object are his fellow human beings, who are therefore seen only from outside, that is, as officials. On the other hand, Josef K. is himself an official; and K. in *The Castle* is known to the other characters merely as "the landsurveyor," as an official. As an official in the bank, Josef K. tells himself, he would not have been subject to the arrest, for there he would be under the protection of his office, which distances him from other people just as the judges are distanced from the accused Josef K. In the bank he is a part of a whole, of a hierarchy just like the organizations of the court; and his personality is absorbed by his function. If, then, the world in the novel is seen from the hero's viewpoint, this viewpoint is not identical with that of the author. Kafka sees the world differently from Josef K., and the latter's value judgments should on no account be taken for those of Kafka himself.

In the seventh chapter Kafka gives us a brief glimpse of his hero from outside, and it becomes clear that the difference between him and the other people, the officials, is not substantive but purely one of viewpoint. From the point of view of his impatiently waiting clients, Josef K. is as much the remote and incomprehensible official as the court functionaries are for him. Concerning what goes on inside a human being, only subjective assertions are possible. Objective contemplation does not penetrate to the human core but is trapped by the official exterior. Therefore no one is justified in judging his fellow man, and therefore, in the priest's view, Josef K. should refrain from judging the doorkeeper. The doorkeeper's mistakes do not justify the failure of the man from the country and the officials' weaknesses do not justify the bad state of Josef K.'s trial: These mistakes are not real but only apparent mistakes, expressive of alienation, of the impossibility of understanding one's fellow man. The many shifting, seemingly contradictory opinions about the doorkeeper advanced by the priest—concerning his conscientiousness and his presumption, his proximity to the law and his ignorance of the law, above all concerning his lack of freedom and the lowliness of his position in relation to the power and dignity of his office—these are no play with paradoxes but are all an expression of the fact that the doorkeeper as a person is unknown and inaccessible to any unequivocal judgment. Only the duty of his office is known, and this consists in forbidding the man from the country to enter into the law. The priest says clearly that the man from the country voluntarily spends his life outside the law. Therefore the blame for his failure is his alone.

Like the man from the country Josef K. is also free, despite his arrest. Kafka makes this clear already in the arrest scene and then again through the priest, for the reason that one can only speak of guilt where there is freedom—and guilt is the theme of the novel. Josef K.'s freedom is confirmed by the explanation of the warders that the court had not pursued him but had been drawn towards his guilt; and again by the remark of the Inspector that he had not come to take K. into custody but only to give him the news of his arrest. The arrest is thus not an action of the court but the state in which Josef K. already finds himself at the outset of the novel. It is a state for which he himself is responsible, but of this he is unaware and does not wish to become aware. Josef K. is not, as he complains, taken by surprise by the court, neither is he held prisoner by it. Even the priest, who belongs to the court, lays no constraint upon him. When K. wants to leave, he is dismissed with the unemotional words: "The Court receives you when you come and it dismisses you when you go." As surprising as this utterance is Josef K.'s reaction: He is disappointed that the priest lets him go without further ado, just as he was earlier by no means delighted when the Inspector told him he could continue living his normal life. He is not happy in his freedom—he does not want the responsibility—and he is dimly aware that a court which does not deprive him of his freedom ultimately cannot acquit him either.

In the legend as in the novel, then, the free man and the unfree official confront one another, and in both cases the man would like to shrug off his responsibility onto the official. The question as to why he attempts this leads into the heart of Kafka's thinking. He answers it in a brief and stylistically unclear passage, which, however, speaks unambiguously to the point at issue:

> Since the Fall we have been essentially equal in our capacity to know Good and Evil; nevertheless it is precisely here we look for our special merits. But only on the far side of this knowledge do the real differences begin. The contrary appearance is caused by the following fact: nobody can be content with knowledge alone, but must strive to act in accordance with it. But he is not endowed with the strength for this, hence he must destroy himself, even at the risk of in that way not acquiring the necessary strength, but there is nothing else he can do except make this last attempt. . . . Now this is an attempt he is afraid to make; he prefers to undo the knowledge of Good and Evil (the term "the Fall" has its origin in this fear); but what has once happened cannot be undone, it can only be made turbid. It is for this purpose that motivations arise. The whole world is full of them: indeed the whole visible world is perhaps nothing other than a motivation of man's wish

to rest for a moment—an attempt to falsify the fact of knowledge, to try to turn the knowledge into the goal. (*Dearest Father*, pp. 43–44).

According to Kafka, the myth of the Fall expresses the fact that man is endowed with a clear understanding of good and evil. His sins derive, not from his ignorance of what he should do, but from his lacking the strength to act in accordance with his knowledge. Thus Kafka makes responsible for man's sinful, fallen state not the eating at the tree of knowledge but the failure to eat at the tree of life (*Dearest Father*, p. 43), which would have given man the strength to act according to his understanding. In Kafka's world, man's basic affliction is his weakness. But he cannot admit this to himself, since he lacks the Christian faith in the forgiveness of sins. Between the perfection of understanding on the one side and the lack of strength on the other, man finds himself in such a desperate situation that he tries, since he cannot increase his strength, to reduce and obscure his understanding. This obscuring of the understanding is advanced by man's attempts to shift the responsibility for his actions from himself to his circumstances, to his fellow men, and to the world in general. This kind of self-justification Kafka calls "motivation." When he says that the whole visible world is nothing but a motivation of man, he means, therefore, that man seeks to evade the torments of his conscience by projecting his own sinfulness onto the external world and representing it as evil and hostile. The "trial" is this life made up of self-defense and self-justification—a trial which must necessarily be lost, for there is no acquittal from human sinfulness. The courts before which Josef K. wants to defend himself, with their appendage of servants and women whose help he seeks, must not be understood as representatives of the divine law—their corruption would render this an absurdity—and also not as an image of the world's wickedness, justifying and excusing the hero's behaviour—as such they would be insignificant for Kafka—but rather as modalities and structures of the human self-justification that arises from weakness; only thus is their incompetence and corruption to be understood.

It is striking how confined the world of the "trial" is and how, in spite of its immediacy, its so-called "realism," it gives the impression of unreality. The reason for this peculiarity lies in the fact that it is a subjective world, built out of the "motivations" of a guilty man. At certain points this is quite clearly stated. When Josef K. asks which staircase will lead him to the Court of Inquiry, he answers his own question in such a way that whichever one he chooses is the one that leads him to the goal. And when he pretends to be looking for a joiner called Lanz and inquires after him, the woman understands the false question correctly and opens the door to the Court of Inquiry. The stair to the dirty, airless attics literally looms up before K.'s questing gaze. He creates his own "visible world" out of his self-justifications: He, not the court, locates the interrogation in the suburban tenement house which is dirty and degenerated like his own inner being; and he himself turns the court's employees into what they are—weak, ignorant, corrupt officials. Kafka repeatedly expressed the opinion that man is molded by his fellow men into the shape of what they see in him. He fought against this "fixing" of himself by others, and he felt himself guilty of the same behavior in relation to others—for example, his parents. "Evil" in the world thus has several aspects: It is the "motivation" of one's own weakness; it is the projection of one's own guilt and narrow-mindedness onto one's surroundings; and it is, as our analysis of officialdom has shown, the expression of the fact that the world confronts us as strange and incomprehensible and that we encounter human beings only as functionaries.

Like the court officials for Josef K., the doorkeeper is a "motivation" for the man from the country. In the doorkeeper's prohibition he finds the excuse for the non-attainment of his goal. But the doorkeeper's role is a double one. He does not only forbid entry, he also, merely by existing, draws attention to it. And at the end Kafka puts into the doorkeeper's mouth the words unlocking the meaning of the entrance to the law, namely that this entrance is intended specifically for the man from the country. In this explanation, the last sentence of the legend, reside the climax and the solution of the puzzling parable—and also the key to the novel itself. The fact that the entrance is intended only for one individual person proves that it does not lead to a universal, generally valid law, comprehensible by reason and accessible to any rational person of good will. No one else ever comes to the gate that is intended for the man from the country; and the doorkeeper himself has no access to the law, which is the law of the man from the country. The law in question here is the law of each individual, and with regard to it the doorkeeper's paradoxical attitude, both forbidding access and drawing attention to it, makes sense; for man attains to his own law as he attains the highest court—which is identical with the act of self-judgment—not by following procedures but by staking his whole being, in defiance both of all outward circumstances and of his own wishes. This law is reminiscent of Nietzsche's law, of which Zarathustra says: "Can you impose on yourself your own criteria of good and evil, suspending your own will above yourself like a law? Can you be your own judge and the avenger of your own law? It is terrible to be alone with the judge and avenger of one's own law." That Nietzsche's and Kafka's law applies only to oneself makes it no less uncompromising and transcendental. It gains its validity not through its universality but through its unconditional claim on the self, which allows man no rest but drives him his whole life long to achieve the impossible—in spite of the doorkeeper's prohibition on striving toward it, in spite of the diversions of the worldly authorities, above all in spite of the secret longing, born of weakness, to evade it. One's fellow man cannot help towards an understanding of this law, which is identical with an acknowledgment of guilt. It is expressly stated in the novel that only the individual can achieve anything before the court and that lawyers' assistance is not allowed. Neither the support of women, nor the lawyers' learned arguments, nor a justification worked out in detail by Josef K. of his entire life, can affect the trial favorably, for the law is uncompromising and cannot be influenced by any defense, which must always be based on extenuating circumstances. For this reason it is said that the court is inaccessible to arguments.

The doorkeeper has been interpreted as the representative of the world, which, it is asserted, blocks man's entry into the law. But this is to align oneself with Josef K. rather than with Kafka. It is true that the world is no more likely than the doorkeeper to usher man into the law, but it is also not capable of sealing his entrance to the law. All interpreters of the text agree, says the priest, that the doorkeeper cannot close the gate. This means that even though the doorkeeper forbids entry, he cannot ultimately prevent it. Access to the law is thus not dependent on the world and the doorkeeper in either a positive or a negative sense. The man from the country does not attain the law even in death, anymore than Josef K. attains his judge or the Hunter Gracchus attains the afterlife. And the hunger-artist is the very opposite of an apotheosis of asceticism. Emancipation from the world does not in itself lead to the law; guilt is not eradicated by death—in this Kafka follows the Judeo-Christian tradition—but rather it survives K. in the form of shame.

The necessity to which the doorkeeper, like all officials, is subject, and which is discussed by the priest, must be understood not as an expression of the law, but as the deprivation and limitation of the fallen world. The priest emphasizes that what the doorkeeper says is necessary but not true. Josef K. ignores this when he declares that lying has been turned into a universal principle. And Kafka's interpreters have also failed to note this remark when they identify the worldly authorities as representatives of a cosmic order. *The Trial* implies neither an idealistic interpretation of the world as the realization of truth, nor a view of the world ruled by determinism, which knows only the automatic sequence of cause and effect but does not recognize guilt. Kafka is equally far removed from a critique of his age or his society. After Josef K., at his first interrogation, has concluded his speech of accusation against the court, the Examining Magistrate points out to him that he has, with his speeches, deprived himself of the advantage of a first examination: Instead of exploring his inner self, he has criticized the external world. K.'s accusing words constitute, then, not a valid criticism of the authorities, but a cover-up of his own guilt, a "motivation," and a useless self-justification. Kafka stated, not only implicitly in his works but also explicitly, that he felt himself called to be not the critic but the exponent of his age (*Dearest Father*, pp.

99–100; *Diaries* II, p. 206). His critique is directed always at himself. This self-judgment is the dynamic element in almost all his works, from the first successful story "The Judgment," which gave him deep satisfaction, to the late novella "A Hunger-Artist," in which he exposed his own flight from the world, his propensity to asceticism, and the source of his art.

Kafka was no truth-seeker in the sense of striving for an absolute, universal truth. He regarded such knowledge as impossible. In his notes he speaks at one point of "two kinds of truth": the truth which is gained by eating at the tree of knowledge, and which is the knowledge of good and evil; and the truth which is represented by the tree of life and which is goodness itself. This truth is given us only in glimpses; we cannot know it, since it is a whole and not divisible into subject and object. By contrast, Kafka believed that we are born with the knowledge of good and evil, and hence of our guilt; and that it is entirely up to us to take this knowledge upon ourselves. Thus the one avenue to truth is, for him, the consciousness of guilt; for to become identical with the truth (and this is the only way to grasp truth as goodness) has been rendered impossible for man through the Fall—through the fragmentation into truth and lie, good and evil, subject and object. Just as there is for Kafka no identity of perceiving subject and perceived truth, so there is for him no theological certainty through a mystical union with God. God is for Kafka "the absolutely Other," and man is even separated from him in a double sense: "The Fall separates us from him, the tree of life separates him from us." To this God there is no relationship except that of antithesis and insuperable separation, which is expressed in human consciousness of guilt. Consciousness of guilt, then, must not be interpreted psychologically in Kafka, but must be understood in its central religious significance. Just as Kierkegaard declares that the human bond with God is repentance, so Kafka sees the only path to the "law" or the "highest judge" in the acknowledgment of guilt. And, like Kierkegaard, he, too, knows the anguish which overcomes man at the knowledge of his guilt and the encounter with his judge. Hence the entrance to the law is guarded not only by the one, still friendly, doorkeeper but also by other, more powerful ones, of whom even the first doorkeeper is afraid. It is partly anguish that finally kills Josef K.: Being strangled is always an expression of anguish in Kafka, and to die from anguish is to "die like a dog."

Josef K. has not understood the meaning of the parable. Kafka expresses this by an image: The light which the priest gives to Josef K. is extinguished in his hand. Fear of acknowledging his guilt and the human desire to lead a quiet life outside the trial have prevented him from hearing what the priest meant to tell him by means of the legend: that he should give up his evasions and confront his judge. He has not, however, wasted his life on the outside, like the man from the country, the worldly-wise non-fool. Once he is told of his arrest, once he recognizes the procedure, he can no longer break out of the trial in ceaseless motion—the anxiety of conscience. His feeling of guilt torments him, but it ennobles him also and beautifies him, just as all the accused, even the cringing and servile Block, are beautiful in the eyes of the women. Only the girls around the cynic Titorelli cannot recognize the inner beauty, which derives from proximity to the court and the law.

Although Josef K.'s conviction of his innocence is shattered and he sees that he cannot achieve an acquittal, he is not ready to confess his guilt. Thus he vacillates between the two possibilities suggested by Titorelli, ostensible acquittal and indefinite postponement. Ostensible acquittal is the relief a man brings himself through incessant self-defense and self-justification. Since it is not a real acquittal it leads to ever renewed crises. Indefinite postponement is the displacement of the consciousness of guilt: This response confines not only the trial but also man himself to his lowest level. Since neither of the two possibilities means a release from the accusation, the trial continues until it culminates in the judgment, or, as it is phrased in Kafka's diary, until the condemned man gives up resisting the judgment—until the goddess of justice hunts him down and anguish finally overwhelms and throttles him, and the sting of sin thrusts through his heart.

The question of how the novel would have ended if the hero had behaved otherwise at a decisive point is meaningless in a traditional novel. Character and fate are, at least in a good novel, so intertwined that there is no other possibility for either the decision or the ending; for the author is concerned with the unique, individual case, not with the proliferation of different possibilities of existence. In Kafka's novels the situation is quite different. Here, the hero is a man without qualities, and in place of the fate which confronts man and gives his life a definite direction, the Kafka hero is thrust into an unavoidable conflict; moreover, this always occurs suddenly and without specific cause. It is not that his situation has suddenly changed—Kafka always presents a fundamental condition of human existence—but rather that the hero suddenly understands his situation. This situation is not straightforward but paradoxical, in *The Trial* as in Kafka's other works. Like the hero of "A Hunger-Artist," who wants to live on hunger; like the animal in "The Burrow" who, seeking security, perishes from anguish; like the landsurveyor, who believes himself summoned yet can gain no confirmation of that summons—so, too, Josef K. finds himself in a paradoxical situation. He is accused, perhaps even already condemned, without knowing the accusation or the judge. In a paradoxical situation, man has two possible responses. The paradox can appear to him as a dead end, a trap which he cannot evade. Then man gives himself up for lost, even though he at first strives to free himself. The paradox can, however, also appear to him as a task; he is then impelled to try to transcend his situation. Kafka portrayed these possibilities in two parables. The state of being lost in the contradictoriness of the finite world is treated in the parable of the mouse. To the mouse, who complains that her path between narrow walls is leading her inexorably into a trap, the cat behind her answers that she need only change direction—and eats her up. In our parable, on the other hand, the contradiction between the prohibition and the fact of the door intended only for the man from the country directs us beyond the finite world. It is no accident that Kafka puts the parable in the mouth of a priest who presents it in the cathedral, in place of a sermon.

In the parable, then, Josef K. is shown an alternative mode of behavior: He could transcend his situation by confronting it; he could acknowledge the accusation, instead of trying to justify himself; he could submit to the court, instead of evading the issue through "motivations," just as the man from the country could have entered the law despite the prohibition. But even if Josef K. had followed this course, he would have perished anyway; for man lacks the strength necessary to bear the knowledge of his guilt, as Kafka's comment on the Fall clearly states. Knowledge is just as ambiguous as life itself; it "is both step towards eternal life and obstacle in the way of it. If, after gaining knowledge, you wish to attain to eternal life, then you will have to destroy yourself, the obstacle, in order to build the step, which is the destruction." Despite its destructive effect knowledge must be affirmed, for only through the knowledge of his guilt, only as the judge of himself—never through his actions—can man free himself from his guilt and gain the strength for eternal life. This is what Kafka means when, at the age of 28, he notes in his diary: "This morning, for the first time in a long time, pleasure at the image of a knife being turned in my heart." Or later: "Happiness consisted in the fact that the punishment came and that I welcomed it so freely, happily and with such conviction." The hunger-artist finds the necessary strength through the confession of his deception and dies in the redemptive conviction that he is now truly fasting, that is, fulfilling the meaning of his life. In the "Penal Colony" the destruction which is wrought by the knowledge of guilt is represented by the etching of the offense into the flesh of the guilty; and the strength gained through this knowledge is revealed in the transfigured expression of the dying. Had Josef K. confessed his guilt, then he would not have died like a dog, but would at the end have possessed the strength to execute the judgment himself, like Georg Bendemann in "The Judgment." Since he cannot summon the courage to confess guilt, his strength suffices only to accept the judgment and to cease resisting it. He bows to the court. But his destruction, the execution by the court's two emissaries, is no step toward eternal life.

Interpreters who seek to free Kafka from the reproach of nihilism by searching for a possible salvation for his heroes or even for the possibility of a "happy ending" to his novels must consider that according to Kafka man is himself the obstacle to his salvation during his life. Indeed, living is virtually identical with being this obstacle. We read in the notebook entitled "He": "He has the feeling that he is blocking the path by virtue of being alive. From this blockage he then derives the proof that he is in fact alive." The man from the country and Josef K. succumb to the illusion that the doorkeeper and the authorities are the obstacle to the law, instead of seeking it within themselves. This illusion is to blame not so much for their botched life as for their botched death. "Our salvation is death, but not this one," notes Kafka. This one, the false death, is only a "game"—and it is as a game, as a kind of comedy, that death is portrayed in *The Trial*. For Kafka, death was neither the final end nor a release. Rather, he believed, in Rilke's phrase, that death must be achieved, that we must grow in the strength to die. The mode of dying is therefore of fundamental significance in his works. The "Penal Colony" deals with almost nothing else; and in Kafka's notes we find many descriptions of dying, some of them sketches for the conclusion of *The Trial*. Because the conception of this novel demanded from the outset a particular ending, even a specific mode of dying, Kafka was able to write the final chapter, whereas his other novels and many stories lack an ending. Even though *The Trial* remained a fragment and we are probably without precisely those chapters that precede the last one, we can yet understand from the parable why Josef K., lacking the strength to die, must succumb to a dog's death. No interpretation which understands the legend correctly and recognizes that the man from the country decays into a wretched end without gaining admission to the Law can regard Josef K.'s salvation as possible.

The fact that there is no salvation for his heroes and that their end does not signify their entry into the law does not, however, imply that Kafka was a nihilist. Gerhard Kaiser asserts that, of the tradition of "negative theology," only the negative has survived in Kafka. This I cannot accept, for with Kafka, as in negative theology, the negative points to a positive: The lie points to truth, the consciousness of being trapped to a glimpse of freedom, and the unavoidable feeling of guilt to the necessity of the law. The positive itself—truth, freedom, the law—was to be sure never directly portrayed by Kafka. He was no symbolist of the metaphysical, as he is understood by Max Brod and his school; neither was he a symbolist of "negative transcendance," as Erich Heller claims. He described the paradox of existence and the suffering it generates, not for its own sake, but as tasks imposed by life. Like Josef K., who basically knows it although he will not admit it to himself, Kafka was aware that the world's misery and evil accused *him* and declared him guilty. Because he felt himself guilty he subjected his heroes to the law. In contrast to most confessional novels, Kafka's works are neither the apologia of the hero nor that of the author, but rather a judgment on himself. This demands a new attitude from the reader. He must not naively identify with the hero, as Josef K. identifies with the man from the country; for then he falls into the further error of Josef K. (into which in fact many readers and critics repeatedly do fall) of indicating the negativity, absurdity, and devilishness of the world, instead of "endorsing the world" and carrying out the judgment on oneself, as Kafka insists.

In *The Trial*, Josef K.'s arrest is presented novelistically as an event; his attempts to free himself from the arrest through self-justification are described as moves and counter-moves which Josef K. pursues in the course of a year; and the failure of these efforts seems caused by the resistance of the world, the inadequacy of the officials, and their ignorance of the law. The parable, on the other hand, stripped of all novelistic elements, portrays the arrest as that which it in fact is, namely a fundamental human situation: Anguish arrests man before the open door to the law and does not permit him to enter. His failure is already included in this situation. The explanation for the failure, which in the novel lies in the world and in other people, is in the parable reduced to the one doorkeeper. Through this concentration on the essential elements and through the reduction of an event to a situation rendered transparent through imagery, the legend becomes the key to the novel, indeed not only to the novel but to all of Kafka's works. For example, we are now struck by the fact that, in *The Castle* as well, the time sequence is insignificant and that the various undertakings of the landsurveyor represent not progress but repetitions of a single unchanging effort. Here, too, the events are thus only novelistic portrayals of a fundamentally unalterable situation. The world *qua* world of the officials is identical in the two novels and one must presume that it has the same function in both works, namely to reflect man's attitude to the world and to himself, and not to reproduce an external reality or to serve as criticism of society or of the age. The appearance of men in their function as officials or employees, or at least as representatives of a profession that submerges their humanity, occurs again and again in Kafka. The absence of a time dimension and the description of events as a mere means of portraying a specific situation in narrative form is common to all of Kafka's works. Although there is in them no development of the hero and no progress of the action towards a conclusion, Kafka's works do not lack tension. This lies, to be sure, not in the narrative movement, as with a traditional story, but in the situation itself. There is no tension in the outcome, but a tension between opposites. Kafka never tried to reconcile these opposites or to dissolve the paradox and with it the tension, for he would thereby have robbed his works of their true substance. Their fragmentary form is thus no accident, but an appropriate expression of the content of Kafka's works. Even stories with a conclusion like "A Country Doctor" and "In the Penal Colony" are not in their essence any more rounded off than *The Castle*, "The Giant Mole," or

"The Burrow." The fascination exercised by Kafka's work consists precisely in the fact that it offers neither solutions nor answers but only questions—questions that the reader senses apply to himself, even if he does not always understand how. In a little parable Kafka tells of a man who is subjected to an examination: He can answer none of the questions, and therefore—he passes the examination.

The Opaqueness of *The Trial*

by Walter H. Sokel

... Unlike the earlier punitive fantasies, *The Trial* does not specify the guilt for which its protagonist is arrested. The Court that judges Josef K. withholds the clear message given, in the earlier works, by father and family. Indeed, the confrontation of the self with its judge fails to take place. Punishment and annihilation remain; but understanding and atonement are gone.

The physical circumstances of Josef K.'s death reflect its subjective meaninglessness. Whereas Georg Bendemann dies in broad daylight, in the center of life, and Gregor Samsa departs with the first gleam of dawn, Josef K. is knifed in darkness and silence on the deserted periphery of his city. The external darkness surrounding him has its complement in the darkness within him. He does not understand his death. As he fails to see his judges, so he fails to recognize himself. He does not discern within himself a conviction certain and firm enough to be his truth. His inner self remains as unfathomable as the Court.

The Trial is the only truly opaque work among the major writings of Kafka. Its opaqueness results from two factors: the total ambiguity of the Court and the total ambivalence of its hero.

If we understand that the Absolute had two distinct faces for Kafka, we shall do greater justice to his complexity than if we dismiss it as pure paradox. We might define these two aspects of the Absolute by attaching the name of Plato, a philosopher Kafka held in high esteem, to one and the name of Jehovah to the other. With its Platonic face, the Absolute was pure spirit and the physical world illusion; engagement in it was fatally wrong. With its other face—the face of Jehovah, behind whom the features of Kafka's robust and vital father lurked—it was energy and incessant will, a stream of generations and unending continuity of life. From this ambiguity within the Absolute, it followed that the self would become guilty in two opposite directions. It would become guilty before the

"The Opaqueness of *The Trial*" [editor's title], from *Franz Kafka*, by Walter H. Sokel, pp. 27–32. Copyright © 1966 by Columbia University Press. Reprinted by permission of the author and of Columbia University Press.

Platonic aspect by getting "engaged," not merely sexually but economically and socially as well—by "wanting to snatch at the world with twenty hands," as Josef K. says of himself. On the other hand, the self would become guilty before the creator and progenitor of life by refusing "engagement" in the fullest sense of the word, by keeping itself pure in sterile virginity. In one case, it was the engaged and striving façade, in the other, the celibate true self that sinned and had to be sacrificed. The fate of Georg Bendemann shows the former, the fate of the misogynist officer of *The Penal Colony* or of the chaste sister of Barnabas in *The Castle* shows the latter guilt. *The Trial*, however, begun under the immediate shattering impact of Kafka's first break with his fiancée, Felice Bauer, illumines the double and, consequently, total guilt of the self. In Josef K.'s Court the two faces of the Absolute combine to form the enigmatic mask of total ambiguity.

There is a further reason for the novel's ambiguity. It is Josef K.'s inability to decide between the forces battling within him. In Josef K., an unacknowledged *homo religiosus* clashes with the consciousness of economic man. His official impulse of self-preservation and self-assertion resists the upsurge of his unofficial religious impulse, the craving for self-surrender and self-transcendence, objectified by his arrest. It is of highest significance that the Court comes closest to him and appeals to him most directly through a priest. The protagonists of *The Judgment* and *The Metamorphosis* were arrested by the submerged childhood of self within them. In Josef K. the submerged childhood of man, rather than of the individual, arrests the apparently emancipated façade of modern rationality.

By naming his protagonist Josef and adding the name Josef to the initial K. of his own name, Kafka might have hinted at this vertical split in himself and modern man. The "Josefstown" district of Prague, on the edge of which he had been born, had in his childhood still been the site of the ghetto and the center of criminal life. As he once remarked to Gustav Janouch, the new "Josefstown," with its broad streets and bright, airy buildings, presented only a "cover-up" surface, beneath which the dark, filthy, and frightful alleys of the ghetto lay merely submerged.

The careful reader becomes aware of this division within Josef K. Verbally, he seems to fight for reason, for man as defined by the rational legal system of the modern state, and denies the possibility of any extra-legal guilt. By his acts, however, he seeks out and, in the end, submits to the Court. In his mind he never comes to a clear decision for either one or the other. Consequently, the inner truth can never come to light. His conflicting pulls toward surrender, which would give meaning to his death, and toward resistance, which denies meaning to it, tear the whole concept of a true self apart. To be sure, the pull toward surrender and death does prove stronger. For K. lets himself be executed. He even awaits his executioners and leads them toward his place of execution. His consciousness, however, to the last, withholds definitive assent.

The total ambivalence of the hero becomes the total ambiguity of the story. To appreciate the full extent of this ambiguity, we merely have to compare the last thoughts of Georg Bendemann and Gregor Samsa with the last thought of Josef K. Their last thoughts express not only assent to their death but also affirmation and affection for life as embodied in their families. The last thought of *The Trial*, however, is "shame." Shame, it seems, will survive the protagonist. This final noun of the novel not only emphasizes a desperate negativity in contrast to the tragic affirmation with which the earlier punitive fantasies ended; it also expresses a total ambiguity, which makes it impossible to decipher the final meaning of *The Trial*. For it is entirely uncertain to what the noun "shame" refers. It could refer to Josef K.'s failure to resist his execution, or to the senselessness of his murder, and to the shamefulness of a court that orders such injustices. In either case, "shame" would express Josef K.'s mental defiance coexisting with his physical submission. However, it could also refer to his refusal to kill himself or to understand what the Court expects of him. Then the novel would have the opposite meaning. Josef K. would be justly punished for his stubborn rejection of the possibility of his guilt. Both interpretations are equally justified even though contrary to each other. The unrelieved ambiguity of *The Trial* dissolves, therefore, not only the idea of a true self but also the possibility of discerning a truth altogether.

This ambiguity of the work reflects not only the ambivalence of the character but also the ambivalence of the author. In its last thought the consciousness of the character has become the comment of the narrator. It was Kafka himself who could not come to a decision about the meaning of his novel. He excised passages that would have shown Josef K.'s craving to be united with the Court or his longing to be transfigured in death, and would have made him resemble the officer of *The Penal Colony*. Kafka crossed out a reverie of Josef K. which would have been the opposite of his actual death in the novel's final scene. In that passage Josef K. succeeds in entering the court house whence the warrant of his arrest had been issued, and he experiences a transfiguration, symbolized by a new garment of perfect fit. By eliminating this radiant vision from the novel, that is, from the consciousness of his protagonist, Kafka himself enacted the process of repression which his hero is engaged in. Josef K. exhibits tendencies toward surrender and suicide which form the powerful subterranean drift that counteracts his ever conscious intention and action and pulls him ever further along toward destruction. These persist subliminally in fleeting thoughts, gestures, and unreasoned acts, to which Josef K. seems to be driven. Except for the initial arrest, it is always Josef K. who either actively seeks or welcomes contact with the Court. Josef K.'s longing for contact with the Court emerges perhaps most clearly in the Titorelli chapter. Josef K. rejects the painter's suggestions for compromise solutions and insists on absolute acquittal by the highest Judges. His insistence amounts to a full recognition of their supreme authority over him and, beyond that, implies his wish to be accepted and approved by them. This is the limit to which Kafka allows K.'s wish for the Court to become conscious.

In his preceding works Kafka revealed the strategies of repression his heroes engaged in and let the truth be said. In writing *The Trial* he imitated his character and threw out anything that might reveal him directly and unambiguously. In the process of creating his protagonist, Kafka himself performed the activity that constituted his character. He excised and refused to show the "whole truth." Consequently he expunged dreams that would have betrayed Josef K. to himself and to the reader. In *The Castle*, where he deals with a hero much more conscious of his purposes, Kafka leaves K.'s dream in the text and also allows him a revealing childhood memory.

The reasons for Kafka's excisions in *The Trial* are twofold. For one thing they show that he desired to make so complete the division between the conscious surface and the subterranean level in his protagonist's character that Josef K. would be utterly unaware of one level of himself and the reader would be unaware of what compelled Josef K. toward his destruction. Josef K. thus became the precise image of the modern Central European bourgeois who, in our century, would be caught unawares by the eruption of destructive irrationalism around him; yet the tendencies that made this possible were to be found within the bourgeois himself. In this respect Kafka's own art did what he ascribed to the art of Picasso: it portrayed the distortions of reality that had not yet entered consciousness. Secondly Kafka, at the stage of *The Trial*, could no longer bring himself to condone his hero's conscious assent to the judgment that would destroy him.

Gesture and Posture as Elemental Symbolism in Kafka's *The Trial*

by Karl J. Kuepper

In an earlier version of one of the last passages in *The Trial* Josef K. actually cries out: "I have to speak. I raise my hands."[1] In the final version of the same passage the apparent slip of the author is eliminated, Kafka re-assumes his usual narrative position and returns to the past tense and the third person singular: "He raised his hands and spread out all his fingers" (p. 286). It must be that Kafka, for a moment, loses his epic distance and thus identifies with his main character.[2] This is later changed for reasons of consistency, but somehow Kafka compensates for the obvious loss of immediacy: Josef K.'s gesture becomes more detailed and expressive.

That Kafka was preoccupied with gestures has been pointed out several times. Walter Benjamin was the first one to draw attention to their great significance in Kafka's work.[3] For Benjamin the sudden and unexplained appearance of gestures reflects the alienation between man and his body. Gestures assume a life of their own and point to the symbolic context of the theater which is continuously present in all of Kafka's novels. Fritz Martini, in his excellent interpretation of an episode from *The Castle*, also sees the gestures in direct relationship to the theatrical setting, in this instance the court-yard of the *Herrenhof*.[4]

Other critics, such as Heinz Hillmann, Walter Sokel, and Gesine Frey, nearly always try to find unequivocal meaning in the particular gesture

From *Mosaic*, vol. III, no. 4 (Summer 1970), pp. 143-152. Copyright © 1970 by the University of Manitoba. Reprinted by permission of the editor of *Mosaic*.

[1] Franz Kafka, *The Trial*, trans. Willa and Edwin Muir, definitive edition, revised 1957 (New York, 1965). Hereafter all quotations from this text are identified only by the page numbers in brackets.

[2] Cf. Friedrich Beissner, *Der Erzähler Franz Kafka*, 4th ed. (Stuttgart, 1961), about the consistent narrative perspective in Kafka's work.

[3] Walter Benjamin, *Schriften*, Vol. II (Frankfurt, 1955), especially pp. 207-209, 213, 217 and 226.

[4] Fritz Martini, *Das Wagnis der Sprache*, 2nd ed. (Stuttgart, 1956), cf. especially pp. 298 and 330.

under discussion.[5] In this way they undoubtedly gain important insights into the novel as a whole but neglect to do justice to the complexity of the situation in which that gesture has a major function. Sokel, for example, clearly has a point when he explains that Josef K. is basically an ambivalent character. He fails, however, to see that the ambivalence encompasses every significant motif in the novel, that therefore every move Josef K. makes or tries to make is itself ambiguous. The hero's predicament is thus continuously reflected in each facet of his actions, especially in his gestures.

First, a few examples will show how gestures function within a certain situation. The terms "gesture" and "posture," respectively, will consequently be employed in a rather wide sense, i.e., to comprehend all physical movements or positions of a character which convey a message to his environment. A second group of examples will then serve for an examination of certain related or similar gestures which reappear throughout the novel.

All gestures in *The Trial* have in common that they involve an element of error. So Josef K. clearly misinterprets a situation when he first meets Block. Block, at the door of Huld's house, is standing there in his shirtsleeves and cuts a rather miserable figure. K. therefore feels very confident: " 'Is Leni your mistress?' inquired K. curtly. He was straddling his legs slightly, his hands, in which he was holding his hat, clasped behind his back. The mere possession of a thick greatcoat gave him a feeling of superiority over the meager little fellow" (p. 209). This gesture clearly indicates K.'s attitude, and the comment of the narrator leaves no doubt about its meaning. But whatever makes K. feel superior is obviously only momentary: Block's embarrassing situation and the thick coat (the German original has *stark* which also means "strong") hardly justify K.'s gesture. The ambiguity here is rather subtle: generally speaking K. is of course a much "stronger" character than Block, but the reasons for his self-assurance in this instance are not very convincing.

In the next example taken from the first chapter K. finds himself guarded in his room. Contemplating a possible escape he considers certain decisive movements or gestures and then actually performs others. This contrast reflects to a surprising extent K.'s position in and towards his trial. The two guards offer to get him something to eat: "Without replying to this offer K. remained standing where he was for a moment. If he were to open the door to the next room or even the door leading to the hall, perhaps the two of them would not dare to hinder him, perhaps this would

---

[5] Heinz Hillmann, *Franz Kafka, Dichtungstheorie und Dichtungsgestalt* (Bonn, 1964), pp. 130–136. Walter Sokel, *Franz Kafka, Tragik und Ironie* (München, 1964), cf., especially pp. 227 ff. Gesine Frey, *Der Raum und die Figuren in Franz Kafkas Roman "Der Prozess"* (Marburg, 1965).

be the simplest solution of the whole business, to bring it to a head. But perhaps they might seize him after all, and if he were once down, all the superiority would be lost which in a certain sense he still retained" (p. 11). The ambiguity of the situation becomes apparent in K.'s stopping and pausing. Movement towards the door might very well decide the trial before it has actually begun, especially if one sees it in connection with the doorkeeper parable. This would, however, involve a considerable risk which K. is afraid of taking. The gesture of stopping and pausing, emphasized by the absolute lack of the spoken word, therefore clearly indicates the nature of K.'s predicament. The fact that he eventually retreats to his room and lies down on his bed seems to extend the "pause" of inactive waiting and to generalize its ambiguity.

The third example from the cathedral chapter focuses on the gesture of the church warden, which is truly bewildering for K. Waiting for the Italian business friend inside the cathedral he suddenly feels observed by the church warden, a strange looking figure in a long black garment: " 'What's the man after?' thought K. 'Do I look like a suspicious character? Does he want a tip?' But when he saw that K. had become aware of him, the verger started pointing with his right hand, still holding a pinch of snuff in his fingers, in some vaguely indicated direction. His gesture seemed to have little meaning. K. hesitated for a while, but the verger did not cease pointing at something or other and emphasizing the gesture with nods of his head" (p. 258). In the larger context of this passage the English version employs the term "gesture" several times. To my knowledge, Kafka himself used terms such as *Geste, Gebärde* or even *Mimik* very sparingly, if at all. I could not find a single example in the German original.[6] Ordinarily the raised hand and the tight position of its

---

[6] Franz Kafka, *Der Prozess*, in *Gesammelte Werke*, ed. Max Brod (Frankfurt: S. Fischer Verlag, 1946, reprinted 1963).

fingers would give this gesture a solemn prophetic meaning. But the snuff-box and even more the snuff itself between those fingers create a severe disturbance. The gesture thus becomes highly ambiguous in suggesting both dignity and near baseness.

From the very beginning of his trial, it becomes important for K. to establish connections with other people, in the hope that they can be of help to him in his predicament. He often looks for some form of physical contact, and the gesture of shaking hands occurs so frequently in *The Trial* that it must be seen in a larger context.[7] After the interrogation in the first chapter, K. tries to conciliate the inspector and bring the matter to an end: ". . . he stepped over to the Inspector's table and held out his hand. The Inspector raised his eyes, bit his lips, and looked at K.'s hand

stretched out to him; K. still believed he was going to close with the offer. But instead he got up . . ." (p. 19). For K. this handshake would mean that his arrest was null and void, but the inspector's gesture, which K. interprets as hesitating, actually indicates the embarrassment of a representative of the court at such a thought. Even when K., a little later, offers to shake hands with his landlady, Frau Grubach, he wants to ascertain that the problems his interrogation has raised are settled, and so he asks to hear her opinion or rather judgement, as is mentioned twice: " '. . . your judgement, the judgement of a sensible woman' " (p. 27). He wonders whether she will shake hands with him: " 'The Inspector wouldn't do it,' he thought" (p. 27). But Frau Grubach later forgets to shake hands with him. It is obvious that the trial cannot be ended by a mere gesture, not even in K.'s own mind. The ambiguity seems to lie in the meaning which K. attaches to the handshake as opposed to its possible insignificance as a mere gesture of greeting. This becomes apparent when the clerk in the chanceries offers to shake hands with K.: ". . . he held

---

[7] Physical contacts, especially those in the sexual sphere, play a much greater role in *The Castle*. Cf. W. Emrich, *Franz Kafka* (Bonn, 1958), on the women in Kafka's novels.

out his hand to K., who had not expected that" (p. 75). K. is taken by surprise here; he may not want to establish contact with the clerk. Similarly his uncle's handshake is of dubious value; K. has always considered him a nuisance, and his eagerness to shake hands with his nephew particularly embarrasses K.: ". . . stretching out his right hand from the very doorway, and then thrusting it recklessly across the desk, knocking over everything that came in its way" (p. 114). K.'s uncle appears here to be just as much of a danger to K.'s dignity and position in the bank as the trial authorities and their strange actions. This also throws a doubtful light on the nearly identical gesture of the priest in the cathedral: "The priest stretched out his hand to K. while he was still on the way down from a higher level" (p. 267). Although the priest evokes a feeling of trust and confidence in K., the gesture itself would not appear very significant in view of the other events in the cathedral. In other words, the handshake contains an element of hope for K., but seen in connection with similar gestures in the novel it also reveals that the priest may not be trustworthy.[8]

The ambiguity is even more obvious in another group of gestures, all of them dealing with beards. The fact that many characters in the novel have long beards may point to the fashion orthodox Jews observed in the Prague of Kafka's youth (although K. Wagenbach's biography, especially the photographs published in it, gives hardly any corroboration for this assumption).[9] The thin, sparse beards of some figures take on an important meaning in connection with certain gestures, which will become apparent in the following passages. When Josef K. is brought before the inspector for his first interrogation he looks out of the window into Fräulein Bürstner's room: ". . . behind them, towering head and shoulders above them, stood a man with a shirt open at the neck and a reddish, pointed beard, which he kept pinching and twisting with his fingers" (p. 15). Emrich sees in this gesture and its circumstances a clear expression of sexuality.[10] This is probably justified, for the gesture occurs again when K. is approached by the man-mad woman in the empty courtroom; this time it is Bertold, the student, observing him, but again the beard is sparse and reddish: ". . . a young man . . . strove to add dignity to his appearance by wearing a short, straggling reddish beard, which he was always fingering" (p. 69). The context points to a second aspect of the gesture, the attempt to convey an attitude of either pretended or actual reflection. There is further evidence for this when K. makes his speech in the courtroom and part of the audience reacts in this very typical manner: "A few men in the first

---

[8] Cf. also the rejected passage: " 'Where are you?' 'Here,' said the priest and took his hand" (p. 324).
[9] Cf. Klaus Wagenbach, *Franz Kafka, eine Biographie seiner Jugend* (Bern, 1958).
[10] Cf. Emrich, p. 278.

row pulled at their beards" (p. 53). The buttons they wear identify them as belonging to the court in some way and all have reason to be bewildered—or to be lost in thought. A little later, however, the same beards are described as "stiff and sparse, and to take hold of them would be like forming claws rather than taking hold of beards" (p. 59).[11] Here again the allusions have sexual overtones, further strengthened by the use of the simile "claw." [12]

The connection between sexuality and thought, even if the latter is only pretended, is also apparent in the gestures of Huld, who has the habit of "stroking a strand of hair in the middle of his beard and gazing at the carpet, perhaps at the very spot where K. had lain with Leni" (pp. 142–143). Huld's thought, while fingering his beard, seems to focus directly on the sexual act of K. and Leni, which is of ironic significance with regard to Block. For although Block is described as having a long beard (cf. pp. 209 and 241), he never manipulates it. Instead he is caught by Leni "plucking at the hair of the skin rug lying before the bed" (p. 245). An earlier scene is of similar significance; this time Block, "having blown out the candle," keeps "snuffing the wick with his fingers" (p. 211). The two gestures are obviously related: since Block has a beard but never fingers it—this would point to an attitude of reflection and/or to the sexual sphere—he is not only unable to reflect and concentrate on his trial, but also virtually powerless or even impotent. The shaggy fur or the stiff wick is his surrogate for the beard, the symbol of virility, and in both cases the presence of Leni increases the significance of this ambiguous gesture. It is noteworthy that Gesine Frey interprets these important motifs only on one level; e.g., she refers to Block's humiliation, which neither explains fully his strange behaviour nor links this gesture to similar ones in the novel.[13]

When K. enters the courtroom for his first interrogation, he finds it to be a medium-sized, crowded room with two windows and a gallery running immediately beneath the ceiling. This gallery is so low that the audience can "stand only in a bent posture with their heads and backs knocking against the ceiling" (p. 47). This scene becomes even more grotesque by the fact that some members of the audience "had brought cushions with them, which they put between their heads and the ceiling, to keep their heads from getting bruised" (p. 49). Everyone connected with the trial is forced into a stooping posture at one time or another, the accused in the corridors—"their backs remained bowed" (p. 79)—the whipper in the lumber-room with his two victims, "stooping because of the low ceiling"

---

[11] The translation of this passage is partly mine, as the Muir version misrepresents the German original. Cf. *Der Prozess*, p. 62.

[12] K. calls Leni's hand a "claw" of which Emrich has shown the sexual connotations (Emrich, p. 278).

[13] Frey, p. 121.

(p. 104), and even the canopy over the side pulpit from which the priest later addresses K. is constructed "in such a way that a medium-sized man could not stand upright beneath it but would have to keep leaning over the balustrade. The whole structure was designed as if to torture the preacher" (p. 259). Humiliation and pain are such integral components of all procedures of the trial, that the stooping posture seems like the distinguishing mark of everyone connected or involved with the trial authorities.

This posture of stooping is, however, ambiguous. On one hand, the priest is literally drooping over the balustrade when K. tells him about the undignified behaviour of the court officials, "apparently feeling for the first time the oppressiveness of the canopy above his head" (p. 265): the function of the structure is particularly clear here. On the other hand, the priest on the pulpit actually has to bend down to make his message more specific, to leave no doubt that he is actually addressing Josef K. In other words, this side pulpit is not intended for preaching to a large audience, its purpose is rather to address one particular person, namely Josef K., in private. This explains its existence in the cathedral, where otherwise the main pulpit would have been sufficient. This exclusiveness also characterizes the door leading to the law in the parable: " '. . . this door was intended only for you. I am now going to shut it' " (p. 269). The words of the woman at the door leading to the courtroom sound quite similar: " 'I must shut this door after you, nobody else must come in' " (p. 47). The posture of stooping, besides giving evidence of oppression and humiliation, reflects particularly well the air of exclusiveness, which all communications about the trial seem to have. Titorelli, for instance, bends down to K. to whisper in his ear, "so that the girls outside might not hear: 'These girls belong to the Court too' " (p. 188). Significantly enough, when Titorelli, immediately after this, generalizes his statement and thereby greatly reduces its value for K., he changes his posture: ". . . Titorelli sat down again on his chair and said half in jest, half in explanation: 'You see, everything belongs to the Court' " (p. 188).

The posture of stooping, although ambiguous in itself by referring both to a general humiliation of human beings, as well as to the possibility of personal and exclusive humiliation, has a strange gestic counterpart in the novel, that of looking up and even leaning backwards. So Josef K., in order to match the priest's posture, has "to bend his head far back to see the priest at all" (p. 263). The existence of a father-son relationship is quite evident here, as Walter Sokel has shown.[14] This, however, only in part explains the impact of either posture. It is remarkable that Josef K., before he can actually be executed, is brought into a position which is strongly reminiscent of the one he assumed under the side pulpit in the

---

[14] Sokel, cf. p. 238.

cathedral: "The two of them laid K. down on the ground, propped him against the boulder, and settled his head upon it" (p. 285). The connection between the two scenes, which is established through the related postures, points to the fact that Josef K. is, at the same time, son and sacrifice, and this again throws a special light on the ritual character of the execution and its biblical connotations.

Frequently, communication concerning, and humiliation brought about by the trial itself and its authorities, are unalterably linked together, as in the scene where K. tries to gain information from Block: "The tradesman, who was not only a small man but stooped forward as he sat, spoke so low that K. was forced to bend down to hear every word he said" (p. 224). Often the posture of stooping is essential to gain insight into the trial proceedings, even outside the sphere of oral instruction or conversation. So K. has to bend forward to see the painting in Huld's office (cf. p. 134) just as the man from the country has to peer through the entrance to the law (cf. p. 267). Here, too, insight and self-humiliation are tied together, and this reflects an essential aspect of K.'s position in the trial.

Josef K. attaches extraordinary significance to whether or not a person is sitting or standing in a certain situation. Thus he feels humiliated when he has to stand while the inspector is sitting during the first interrogation. While the narrator describes this scene quite objectively—"the Inspector . . . had crossed his legs, and one arm was resting on the back of the chair" (p. 14)—Josef K. is obviously enraged when he later reports the event to Fräulein Bürstner: "The Inspector is lounging at his ease with his legs crossed, his arm hanging over the back of the chair, like this, an absolute boor" (p. 35). For K. this relaxed sitting position is indicative of an unjustified feeling of superiority. The roles are changed when K. leans back in his chair in the lawyer's office. This time Block is annoyed and points out to K. another meaning of this posture: " 'For if you think you have the advantage of me because you're allowed to sit there at your ease . . . let me remind you of the old maxim: people under suspicion are better moving than at rest, since at rest they may be sitting in the balance without knowing it, being weighed together with their sins' " (p. 239). Block is referring to the allegory of the goddess of justice on whose scales every accused is weighed. K. had earlier made a remark to Titorelli in this context which stands in sharp contrast to Block's opinion: " 'Justice must stand quite still, or else the scales will waver and a just verdict will become impossible' " (pp. 182–183). K. seems to think that the best he can do for his trial is to sit and contemplate, but there is also the possibility that Block is right, that the accused have to become active, even if only to prevent a verdict. In terms of the practical steps to be taken in one's trial the posture of sitting back surely is ambiguous.

On the same level of allegory the dilemma of either sitting back or moving reappears in a striking and significant way on the paintings in

Titorelli's studio and Huld's office, respectively. As mentioned above, K. has to bend forward to distinguish the features on the painting in Huld's office:

> It represented a man in a Judge's robe; he was sitting on a high throne-like seat, and the gilding of the seat stood out strongly in the picture. The strange thing was that the Judge did not seem to be sitting in dignified composure, for his left arm was braced along the back and the side arm of his throne, while his right arm rested on nothing, except for the hand, which clutched the other arm of the chair; it was as if in a moment he must spring up with a violent and probably wrathful gesture to make some decisive observation or even to pronounce sentence. (p. 134)

As far as the posture and the intended gestures of the judge are concerned, their description could hardly be more exact and, in addition, the situation represented on the painting points to the decisive moment before the end of a trial.

The picture of a judge, hanging in Titorelli's studio, is mentioned as being very similar to Huld's. Yet on closer inspection it appears that the resemblance is primarily based on the postures and gestures of the judges:

> True, this was quite a different Judge, a stout man with a black bushy beard which reached far up on his cheeks on either side; moreover the other portrait was in oils, while this was lightly and indistinctly sketched in pastel. Yet everything else showed a close resemblance, for here too the Judge seemed to be on the point of rising menacingly from his high seat, bracing himself firmly on the arms of it. (p. 182)

The few drawings of Franz Kafka published by Max Brod and Klaus Wagenbach give a similar impression: all personal characteristics are missing, movement is all that matters.[15] Note the illustration at the beginning of this article, for example. This raises the question of the possible meaning of these gestures for Josef K. The paintings themselves appear under circumstances that give them a special weight. One emerges from the darkness in the lawyer's office, the other one is somehow unveiled by the painter.

It is quite obvious that the postures and gestures of the judges carry a message for Josef K., and yet, on the other hand, they prove to be no help at all: they are only painted and therefore frozen and static movements. The judges are at the same time moving and resting, sitting back and taking action, which for K. would be impossible to undertake.

The ambiguity of gestures and postures becomes especially clear on this allegorical level, which gives Josef K.'s predicament a certain finality. He actually never seems further away from a judgement than when he assumes a posture similar to that of the judges, i.e., in the chanceries when

---

[15] Max Brod, *Franz Kafka, Eine Biographie* (Frankfurt, 1954); K. Wagenbach, facing p. 130.

he is close to fainting: "K. sat down at once and leaned his elbows on the arms of the chair so as to support himself still more securely" (p. 83). This additional irony clearly indicates the hopelessness of his situation. The gestures of the judges are, as the portraits themselves, only allegorical and thus belong to a sphere which is quite different from K.'s. There is a definite contradiction between this allegory and the "real" world; K.'s experiences with the trial authorities have nothing in common with the idealized portraits. This brings up another stratum of ambiguity: the suggestion of the judges, paradoxical as it is, may very well be intended as a deception for K., a point which has been stressed by Marthe Robert.[16] Although the paintings, through their ambiguous gestures, seem to bear a message for K., all his endeavours must remain futile since the different spheres of allegory and reality contradict each other.

Seen in this light, K.'s failures are necessary in a tragic sense. His inability to make sensible movements is directly related to the ambiguity of each of the gestures discussed and thus reflects K.'s predicament in his trial.

To return to the passage quoted in the beginning, K. will never see this allegorical judge, the court of law cannot even be approached, and what K. has to say remains unheard, in the literal sense of the word; the utterance, in becoming a gesture, becomes also ambiguous—and the gesture itself ends in the very image of despair: "He raised his hands and spread out all his fingers" (p. 286).

[16] Cf. Marthe Robert, *Franz Kafka* (Paris, 1960), especially pp. 116–119.

Kafka and Phenomenology: Josef K.'s Search for Information

by Cyrena Norman Pondrom

Reflecting upon his lifetime efforts to "contemplate the foundations of our existence" the dog of Kafka's "Investigations of a Dog" congratulated himself upon the stir he had caused. "People began to investigate after a fashion, to collect data," he said. "They made a beginning at least, although they are never likely to go farther. But after all that is something. *And though the truth will not be discovered by such means—never can that stage be reached*—yet they throw light on some of the profounder ramifications of falsehood."[1] In that comment, contained in a story written very near the end of his life, Kafka told us much about his method, his insight, and the relationship countless critics would have to Kafka's own efforts to probe "die Fundamente unseres Lebens" (*B*, p. 257). The comment is as applicable to *Der Prozeß* (The Trial) as it is to his much later work, for it should remind us that the world Kafka knew was a world of meaningful appearances of multiple interpretations, of "truth" that could be approached only through falsehood.

A clear understanding of the significance of the dog's observation has several important implications for our approach to Kafka and our interpretation of any single one of his works. First, and fundamentally, it should guide us to see Kafka, not by himself, but in the perspective of one of the important changes in man's way of looking at the world: the view

---

From *Wisconsin Studies in Contemporary Literature*, vol. VIII, no. 1 (Winter, 1967), pp. 78–95. Copyright © 1967 by The Regents of the University of Wisconsin. Reprinted by permission of the editor.

[1] Franz Kafka, "Investigations of a Dog," in *Selected Short Stories of Franz Kafka*, trans. Willa and Edwin Muir (New York, 1952), p. 225; *Beschreibung eines Kampfes*, pp. 261–62; hereafter abbreviated in text as *"B"* (italics mine). Quotations from Kafka's work are taken from a standard translation, but both English and German editions are cited. In a few quotations I have emended the translation to conform to the German diction more literally and have indicated the change by an asterisk before the changed words. All references to Kafka's German texts are from *Gesammelte Werke*, ed. Max Brod (New York). When citing critical studies not available in English, I have quoted the German and placed a translation in the notes.

that man's knowledge of the world is phenomenological. Secondly, it should safeguard us from the kinds of dogmatism in interpretation which have, nevertheless, been one of the constant plagues of Kafka studies. And, finally, it suggests to us an interpretation of *Der Prozeß* which recognizes Kafka's fundamental agnosticism concerning the truthfulness of any single human perception.

Phenomenology itself is the label applied to the method of describing the world that has been theoretically expounded in the twentieth century by Edmund Husserl, a Bohemian Jew who wrote in German, whose exceedingly important first formulations of his philosophy were published in Germany between 1900 and 1913 (that is, at least one year before *Der Prozeß* was begun).[2] It is a philosophy which sees the human consciousness as the foundation, not of the world itself but of the *meaning* of the world, and it emphasizes the ways consciousness and the world are entangled. A close comparison between the assumptions about the way man can know his world evident in *Der Prozeß* and the basic assertions of Husserl will show us, I think, some striking similarities. It is, of course, not a new idea to see Kafka in relationship to some twentieth century philosophical ideas. In fact, Max Bense, in *Die Theorie Kafkas*, provides a useful reminder about the philosophical implications of literature:

> Tatsächlich haben aber nicht nur die positiven Wissenschaften eine Seinsthematik, verfolgen nicht nur sie eine ontologische Tendenz. . . . Auch Literatur, Dichtung, jeder Text—das Thema der Philologie—enthalten eine Seinsthematik, sind zuletzt orientiert an einer ontologischen Tendenz.[3]

And Wilhelm Emrich, in his excellent study of Kafka, includes a section "Denken und Sein: Kafka und Heidegger."[4] But Bense is chiefly concerned to relate Kafka to Heidegger's "Fundamentalontologie" and to see him in the light of the changes in philosophy from Plato to the present, which he has summarized in the opening pages of *Die Theorie Kafkas*.[5] And

---

[2] *Logische Untersuchungen*, Vol. I (1900), Vol. II (1901) "Philosophie als strenge Wissenschaft," *Logos I* (1910–11); trans. Quentin Lauer in *Phenomenology and the Crisis of Philosophy* (New York, 1965). *Ideen zu einer reinen Phänomenologie und phänomenologischen Philosophie*, Vol. I (1913); trans. W. R. Boyce-Gibson, *Ideas* (New York, 1962). References to this work will be given by section number rather than page, to avoid giving references for both German and English editions.

[3] Max Bense, *Die Theorie Kafkas* (Köln, 1952), p. 13. "As a matter of fact, the exact sciences are not alone in having a theory of being, in following an ontological tendency. . . . Literature, poetry, every text—the subject of philology—contain a theory of being and are ultimately oriented in an ontological direction."

[4] Wilhelm Emrich, *Franz Kafka* (Bonn, 1965).

[5] Bense, *op cit*. Bense's unindexed *Die Theorie Kafkas* makes references to Husserl on, for example, pages 19, 27, 61, 64. He clearly sees Kafka's epistemology as phenomenological: "Ich habe shon betont—und es ist dies ja gerade die phänomenologische Lage des kafkaschon Seins—, daß es indifferent ist gegenüber realer oder idealer Gegebenheit." (p. 64) But he treats Husserl simply as a step on the way to Heidegger and, more importantly, he does not

Emrich, who sees Kafka as a *forerunner* of Heidegger, whose *Sein und Zeit* was published in 1927, is careful to distinguish Kafka's views from some of Heidegger's metaphysical assertions. He does not offer us an examination of the parallels between Kafka and Husserl.

In placing Kafka in the context of the twentieth-century novel, it seems to me more useful to examine his epistemological method than his metaphysical conclusions. For whereas the metaphysical and ethical conclusions differ quite sharply in detail from writer to writer, a rather large number of twentieth-century figures share an important body of conclusions about how man knows his world.[6]

If our concern, then, is with epistemological method, Husserl is the most useful touchstone, for in this century he is the seminal thinker for Continental literary and philosophical conceptions of how men know. We need not argue that Husserl is the "source" of Kafka's epistemology; we may observe, simply, that two German-speaking Eastern European Jews both influenced by Christian thought,[7] the one writing philosophy and a decade earlier, the other writing fiction, produced quite similar descriptions of the way man knows his world.

We must recognize Kafka's concern with problems of epistemology as soon as we begin to analyze *Der Prozeß*, for Josef K., by personality and by quest, is a figure absorbed in trying to get some important knowledge. By personality he is one who looks to order, both social and intellectual, for security, one who measures most whom he meets by his own intelligence and who attributes many of his dilemmas to a failure of intellect on the part of a companion. His personality thus leads him both to put a very high value on attaining knowledge and to underestimate the problems of achieving it. During the early stages of his arrest, he speaks of the intellectual poverty of his warders and cites the "senselessness" of suicide as a reason for avoiding it.[8] He fills "with pleasure at having encountered

---

provide a sustained analysis of any single work of Kafka. Instead he uses brief quotations from throughout Kafka's work.

[6] There are, for example, very great differences in the metaphysical insights of Kafka and Camus or Sartre, but there is broad agreement among them concerning man's method of knowing. The agreement about epistemology prompts some important similarities in theme, even where writers do not agree about the metaphysical implications of epistemology.

[7] Kafka was acquainted with Kierkegaard before he wrote *Der Prozeß* and later made an extended study of the Dane; see *Tagebücher*, August 21, 1913. Husserl studied the *New Testament* and converted to Christianity in his twenties; see Herbert Spiegelberg, *The Phenomenological Movement*, Vol. I, 2nd ed. (The Hague, 1965), p. 86.

[8] *The Trial*, trans. Willa and Edwin Muir, rev. by E. M. Butler (New York, 1957), p. 10; *Der Prozeß*, p. 15. All further references to these editions will be abbreviated *T.* and *P.* and will be contained in the text. The German title has connotations missing in the English rendering. As well as the legal meaning, *Prozeß* contains the meanings "operation," "process," and "procedure." In view of the priest's statement "the proceedings only gradually merge into the verdict" ("das Verfahren geht allmählich ins Urteil über"), it seems highly desirable to keep in mind the wider reference of the German title.

a sensible man at last" during his meeting with the inspector (*T*, p. 15; *P*, p. 20) and later belabors that same inspector for not being reasonable. "What kind of man are you, then? You ask me to be sensible and you carry on in the most senseless way imaginable yourself!" he exclaims (*T*, p. 18; *P*, p. 22). In fact, among his more frequent epithets are *dumme* (stupid) which he applies to the duty of inspector (*T*, p. 20; *P*, p. 25), *sinnlose* (senseless) which he applies both to the clerk Kaminer (*T*, p. 32; *P*, p. 36) and to his trial itself (*T*, p. 57; *P*, p. 61), and *verständnislosen* (senseless), with which he describes his executioners (*T*, p. 283; *P*, p. 269). K., we thus observe, sees himself as a reasonable man and demands that the world be the same.

His quest for knowledge or understanding is as clear as his self-conception. In the opening chapter he sets clarity as his first goal: "Any right to dispose of his own things which he might possess he did not prize very highly; *it was far more important to him to become clear concerning his situation" (*T*, p. 7; *P*, p. 12). He continues from the "Who are you?" of his first words to the end of the novel to ask countless questions of all he meets, and he comes to the end of his life with the tormented resolution of a man who has not ceased to value reasonable questions even when they have not been answered. "The only thing for me to go on doing," he thinks, "is to keep my intelligence calm and analytical to the end" (*T*, p. 282; *P*, p. 269).

By such a portrait of Josef K., Kafka's thematic concern with epistemology is inextricably interwoven with both revelation of character and development of plot. K. is something of a superficial phenomenologist himself: he begins investigations and tries to take data. But he holds what Kafka as well as Husserl might well term a "naturalistic misconstruction" (*Ideas*, § 18 ff.). He seeks ideal truth in the empirical world. He can make clear for us Kafka's attitude toward the possibilities of human knowledge less by statement than by example; it is the technqiue of his portrayal and the frustrations of his search for knowledge that are for us the most revealing. The initial description of his consciousness, in fact, shows us the first parallels with Husserl's fundamental ideas.

Husserl's starting point in *Ideas* is the individual consciousness of the world. "Natural knowledge begins with experience (*Erfahrung*) and remains *within* experience," he writes, and goes on:

> to all [the] correct assertions [of every science] there correspond as original sources of the reasoned justification [sic] that support them certain intuitions in which objects . . . appear as self-given and in part at least *given in a primordial (originärer) sense*. . . . To have something real primordially given, and to "become aware" of it and "perceive" it in simple intuition, are one and the same thing. . . . We have primordial experience of physical things . . . of ourselves and our states of consciousness . . . , but not of others and their vital experiences. . . . (*Ideas*, § 1.)

One begins with one's own consciousness, a consciousness neither empty nor simply aware of itself as consciousness, but consciousness *of* something that is part of the world, a something which appears to one as presented from without, self-evident, or in Husserl's word, *Selbstgebung*. In literature, the author may reflect such a starting point by restricting the narrative to the perceptions accessible to a single character. This is precisely what we find in the narration of *Der Prozeß*. "Jemand mußte Josef K. verleumdet haben," goes the now well-known beginning, "denn ohne daß er etwas Böses getan hätte, wurde er eines Morgens verhaftet." It is the matter-of-fact statement of a reasonable man who assumes that cause and effect are inviolable and that everything has an explanation. It is. as we have suggested, precisely the kind of man Josef K. is at the beginning of the novel. Although the syntax is third person, the narrative throughout is restricted to what Josef K. is capable of perceiving. Furthermore, Kafka manages to convey the "primordially given" character of K.'s experience. At this point the explanation for arrest is, "self-evidently" that "someone must have denounced" K., even though he had done nothing wrong. Later, he begins to search the history of his life for the wrongdoing which simply did not exist for him at the beginning of the novel, but this too seems, as it is narrated, self-evidently required of K. Perhaps the clearest example of the way the reader is put completely at the mercy of the point of view of K. comes in the chapter "Lawyer/Manufacturer/Painter." There, within six pages, we are told in the identical accents of completely trustworthy statements:

> But now, when K. should be devoting his mind entirely to work, when every hour was hurried and crowded—for he was still in full career and rapidly becoming a rival even to the Assistant Manager— . . . this was the time when he must sit down to [the] task [of recounting his life]. (*T*, p. 161; *P*, p. 155)

And in contrast:

> And the manager himself? . . . His good intentions would be checkmated, for K.'s waning prestige was no longer sufficient to counterbalance the influence of the Assistant Manager . . . (*T*, pp. 167–68; *P*, p. 161).

In both passages, as elsewhere, the statement of fact is simply declarative: it has the character of the "primordially given." But the perceptions and judgments of other people remain outside this realm. Or slightly to paraphrase *Ideas*, "The other man and his psychical life is indeed apprehended as 'there in person,' and in union with his body, but unlike the body, it is not given to [K.'s] . . . consciousness as primordial." (§ 1) So, during the arrest:

> Yet it occurred to him at once that he should not have said this aloud and that by doing so he had in a way admitted the stranger's right to superintend

his actions; still, that did not seem important to him at the moment. The stranger, however, took his words *in some such sense* . . . (*T*, pp. 4–5; *P*, p. 10; italics mine).

The self-givenness of objects for the individual perception partially helps us to understand the sense of inevitability which accompanies even the most bizarre experience in *Der Prozeß*. It is one of the dream-like qualities of Kafka's narrative that no one demonstrates very much surprise at anything:

> "You are presumably very much surprised at the events of this morning?" asked the Inspector . . . "Certainly," said K., . . . I am surprised, but I am by no means very much surprised" (*T*, p. 15; *P*, p. 20).

Even the arrival of the unexpected executioner is met only by the restrained "So you are meant for me?" (*T*, p. 280; *P*, p. 266). As a result, K.'s demise seems the result of an inexorable process.

However, the sense of inevitability that accompanies the self-given quality of objects[9] in human perception should not lead one to assume that the specific empirical objects are themselves *necessary*. K. makes that mistake. His normal routine seems "necessary" to him, and he is slow to comprehend the fundamental nature of the Court's challenge to that routine. His trial comes to seem necessary to him, in the sense that "necessary" implies special significance in the proceedings being conducted against K. rather than against another. And—as Kierkegaard has reminded us, every man is infinitely interested in his own salvation—from first to last Josef K.'s own life seems to him to be necessary. It is against this last expectation that the words of the priest take on such crushing significance: " 'That means I belong to the Court,' said the priest. 'So why should I want anything from you? The Court wants nothing from you. It receives you when you come and dismisses you when you go' " (*T*, p. 278; *P*, p. 265). K., his routine, and his trial are simply accidental, contingent; the Court in its indifference "receives" them when they appear, "dismisses" them when they go.

In a clearly parallel development of this thought, Husserl explains the accidental nature of specific objects:

> The acts of cognition which underlie our experiencing posit the Real in *individual* form, posit it as having spatio-temporal existence, as something existing in *this* time-spot, having this particular duration of its own and a real content which in its essence could just as well have been present in any other time-spot; posit it, moreover, as something which is present at this

---

[9] Here "objects" may refer to individuals, events, and even processes, such as business routine, trials, or logic. "In our own instance, that of sensory perception, or, in distincter terms, perception of a world of things, the logical individual is the Thing; and it is sufficient for us to treat the perception of things as representing all other perceptions (of properties, processes, and the like)." *Ideas*, § 39.

place in this particular physical shape . . . , where yet the same real being might just as well, so far as its own essence is concerned, be present at any other place, and in any other form. . . . Individual Being of every kind is, to speak quite generally, *"accidental."* It is so-and-so, but essentially it could be other than it is. (*Ideas*, § 2)

But, for Husserl, the contingency of the object does not mean that there is nothing that is necessary. Rather, "it belongs to the meaning of everything contingent that it should have essential being; . . . [that is,] an individual object . . . has its *own proper mode of being*, its own supply of *essential* predicables which must qualify it (*qua* 'Being as it is in itself') if other secondary relative determinations are to qualify it also." (*Ideas*, § 2) In other words, although we assign the world its meaning we do not construct it; the world "is there"; and those qualities of the object that make it what it is are *essential*. And by this reasoning, and on this ideal plane, the essential qualities are *necessary*, for without them the object would not be what it is.

There is, I think, a similar sense in which the events of *Der Prozeß* are "necessary," in which they have an "essential" meaning. And this is the way in which the novel rises to the level of great art—for K. in *Der Prozeß* is an archetypal figure[10] reenacting the mythic search for crucial information which we see throughout western literature. Telemachus sought news of his father; Faust, in knowledge and experience, some information about the limits of human possibility; Job and Josef K., the nature of the charge against them, so they could testify in their own defense. Telemachus, of these the happiest man, sought what he could find on earth. But in all these cases we find a man asking a question or series of questions whose answers he hopes will help to justify his life. In this sense, *Der Prozeß* speaks of what Kafka presents as some of the essential qualities of human experience, without which man would not be what he is: a questioning creature who receives a death sentence, but never discovers the "charges" against him. Or, to put it another way, we perceive the essential features of K. to the extent to which we see him as a symbol of man or a certain kind of man.

But there is an important way in which *Der Prozeß* is different from its non-phenomenological predecessors. For all the other three, the hero is one of a kind; he may represent a type, but his specific identity is of critical importance to the story of his search for information. Telemachus is the son of Odysseus; Job is a good man; and Faust the magus, teacher, scholar of great renown. But Josef K. is a bank clerk; he could just as well have been assistant manager or a tradesman, and his futile attempts to discover the charges against him could have been made as well as by any similar

---

[10] For a discussion of Kafka's use of myth, see Kurt Weinberg, *Kafkas Dichtungen: Die Travestien des Mythos* (Bern, 1963).

man. Job, the good man, is necessary to the supreme test God and the devil design, but K. is "accidental," not needed by the Court, and this is part of the *essential* human experience Kafka portrays. There is added irony in the recognition that, for K., obtaining any *essential* knowledge would have entailed recognizing his own contingency.

Another facet of the essential human experience Kafka describes is the unreliability, uncertainty, and ambivalence of perceptions, despite their immediate presentation as *Selbstgebungen*. When K. shouts at the three who watch his arrest from the window across the way, he turns to observe the inspector, who "was possibly of the same mind, K. fancied. . . . But it was equally possible that the inspector had not even been listening" (*T*, p. 19; *P*, p. 23). Or, in his first interrogation, K. mistakes the crowd for Parties of Left and Right, an audience to be swayed, and only later perceives them all to be officials of the Court (*T*, p. 59; *P*, p. 62). And he speculates in the offices about whether the Court was poor, and thus in a certain sense inferior to him, "though, of course, the possibility is not to be ignored that the money was abundant enough, but that the officials pocketed it . . ." (*T*, p. 74; *P*, p. 76). In fact, most of K.'s experiences in the law offices (chapter three) are completely re-interpreted in the course of his conversation with Kaufmann Block in the eighth chapter. The ambivalence persists to the very end, when, as Heinz Politzer has pointed out,[11] the syntax does not even permit an unequivocal decision about to whom or what belongs the shame which seemed as if it "must outlive him."

The uncertainty and ambivalence are tokens of the way in which man can know his world. He does not receive direct revelations of divine essence and he has no valid appeal past the realm of his own perceptions (which include, scientifically speaking, perceptions of others' perceptions and the synthetic consciousness of these perceptions). Rather, he must found his knowledge upon incomplete, sometimes illusory, perceptions of appearances.

The example Husserl offers is instructive:

> Keeping this table steadily in view as I go round it, changing my position in space all the time, I have continually the consciousness of the bodily presence out there of this one and self-same table, which in itself remains unchanged throughout. But the perception of the table is one that changes continuously, it is a continuum of changing perceptions. (*Ideas*, § 41)

In a very similar sense, K. circles the fact of his trial, keeping it steadily in view as he goes full circle during the cycle of his thirtieth year. The trial remains "there" but his perception of the nature of the trial itself and his relationship to it steadily change. Each perception of the trial must be added to the last perception, and all of them added together yield the

---

[11] *Franz Kafka: Parable and Paradox* (Ithaca, New York, 1962), p. 217.

description of his trial that K. obtains. But in Husserl's words, "The perceived thing in general, and all its parts, aspects, and phases . . . are necessarily transcendent to the perception." (*Ideas*, § 41) However hard K. searches for complete knowledge of the trial, the trial itself transcends his knowledge of it. What he can obtain is a succession of perceptions: he can, it is true, ask others what their perceptions of his trial are. He can unite the perceptions told him by others with his own "primordially given" perceptions into a synthetic consciousness of his trial. But—to use Husserl's terms and yet to expand the analysis strictly in terms of *Der Prozeß*—there are serious limitations, from the standpoint of phenomenological method, upon the possibilities for his knowing adequately the essence of his trial. He is not unlike the astronomer standing on a single planet who attempts to describe the essential features of the universe. The trial is an object which extends at least from the point at which K. recognizes it until the end of his life. Yet at any point at which it is still possible for him to synthesize perceptions, K. has not yet "walked all the way around the table." He has not seen the trial to its end.

Kafka's own preoccupation with this basically epistemological problem is evident from many diary entries during the months just before and during the writing of *Der Prozeß*. One of the clearest appears in *Tagebücher* (Diaries, Vol. I) as an entry for December 17, 1913:

> The truly terrible paths between freedom and slavery cross each other with no guide to the way ahead and accompanied by an immediate obliterating of those paths already traversed. *There are countless numbers of such paths, or only one, it cannot be determined, for there is no vantage ground from which to observe.* There I am. I cannot leave. (Italics mine)

In determining the essential nature of his trial there are more problems for K. than the lack of "a vantage ground from which to observe." One of the most important features of the trial is that it is *K.*'s trial—that is, that it is the trial of the one who perceives it (or, narratively speaking, through whose eyes the reader "perceives" it). In other words, we may suspect that one of the features of the essential being of "the trial" is that it appears as primordially given. Let us for the moment assume, as most but not all critics do, that K. *is* in some sense archetypal, that his trial is representative of the trial of man, or at least of certain kinds of men, and is not simply a category of one. From the phenomenological point of view, K. might seek to determine the essence of his trial by comparing his experience with other men: and in fact he does this with Block the Tradesman. Yet only one's own experience can appear as primordially given; K., or any other single individual, is permanently debarred from verifying "scientifically" this aspect of the nature of the trial of any other. Another may report that his own trial appears to him to be "primordially given." Yet this report must contradict the perceptions of the one he addresses, who observes the other's trial as a fact of the world, but not as primordially given. The two perceptions, instead of reinforcing each other in the manner of scientific data, remain in paradox. So the information Block gives concerning his own trial cannot help K. in determining all the aspects of the "essence of trialness." As a result, the isolation of the individual is increased. One's description of one's own trial always seems different from another's description of his trial. There is no community among the arrested; since only one's own experience appears primordially given, they can give each other little assistance on the problem which most absorbs each: finding out about his trial. Block explained it to K. like this:

> Each case is judged on its own merits, the Court is very conscientious about that, and so common action is out of the question. An individual here and there may score a point in secret, but, no one hears it until afterwards, no one knows how it has been done. So there's no real community, people come across each other in the lobbies, but little is said there (*T*, pp. 218-19; *P*, pp. 210-11).

The means by which K. "knows" his trial and the limitations on that knowledge, incidentally, help us to understand K.'s predicament in seeking help on his trial. At first he rejects all help: "He loathed the thought of chartering anyone, even the most casual stranger, to help him along in this case of his, also he did not want to be beholden to anyone or to initiate anyone even remotely in his affairs" (*T*, p. 42; *P*, p. 47). But later he seeks help almost wherever he can find it, and perversely, he seems in a way to be wrong both times. His initial refusal of help may be seen as a refusal even to permit others to perceive his trial. But if others, like Kaufmann Block, cannot help him much by reports on *their* trials, K. can at least use other people's reports on his own. Since he wants to understand his trial as much as possible, he must use all available "data." He seems to recognize this, and by the time of his encounter with the manufacturer, he willingly uses the information the manufacturer is able to report about K.'s trial. On the other hand, he must also recognize the limits upon the help others can give him; there is no short-cut to understanding and no privileged person can offer revelation. In terms of Husserl's example of the table, no single view of the table is adequate without all the other possible views. Some standpoints may offer a better view than others, just as the painter and priest seem potentially more useful commentators than the lawyer or tradesman, but not even the priest can offer K. anything more than one perception of his situation. Hence, on this level, the priest's approach to K. has epistemological meaning: "You cast about too much for outside help, . . . especially from women. Don't you see that it isn't true help?" (*T*, p. 265; *P*, p. 253).

But despite the warning, K. continues here to seek "too much" outside help, now from the priest. "If the man would only quit his pulpit, it was not impossible that K. could obtain decisive and acceptable counsel from him which might, for instance, point the way . . . toward a mode of living completely outside the jurisdiction of the Court" (". . . zeigen würde . . . wie man auβerhalb des Prozesses leben könnte") (*T*, p. 266; *P*, p. 254). The priest's reproach for such sentiments is as direct as his previous charge that K. sought too much help: " 'With you I can speak openly,' said K. 'Don't be deluded,' said the priest" (*T*, p. 267; *P*, p. 255). There is a similar scene at the end of the chapter:

> "You were so friendly to me for a time," said K., "and explained so much to me, and now you let me go as if you cared nothing about me." "But you have to leave now," said the priest; . . . "You must first see who I am." . . . "You are the prison chaplain," said K. . . . "That means I belong to the Court," said the priest. "So why should I want anything from you? The Court wants nothing from you. It receives you when you come and it dismisses you when you go" (*T*, p. 278; *P*, p. 265).

K. may not even trust the prison chaplain. Although he may use the chaplain's warnings, he still must cope with his own trial by means of his own knowledge;[12] it is humanly impossible for him to have knowledge proceeding from a higher vantage point than the human. Our investigation of epistemological method, then, has led us further toward an understanding of what is symbolized by the court. Earlier we have seen the court, in this passage, revealed as a representative of the essential, indifferent to the comings and goings of the contingent world. A further examination of the same passage suggests that this essential world is also the realm of truth. The priest, who has "explained so much" to K. in the form of the "Legend of the Doorkeeper," can do no more. The multiple interpretations of that ambivalent legend resemble the successive perceptions of the man walking around the table. K. must leave now; but the priest, who has acted in a friendly fashion, makes one last effort to tell K. why it is futile to stay longer. He is the prison chaplain: "That means I belong to the Court." And if the court is the realm of complete knowledge, Truth with the capital letter, the priest *cannot* tell a living K. the truth about his trial. For "Truth" in this sense is instantaneously complete and indivisible, and human perception is time-bound, sequential, and intrinsically unable to achieve the perspective upon itself that could remove it from the realm of time. K. can "collect data," but "the truth will not be discovered by such means."

It is at once K.'s failure and his glory that he does not accept the

---

[12] Should Herman Uyttersprot's re-ordering of the chapters be correct, and the chapter entitled "Block the Tradesman/Dismissal of the Lawyer" follow the chapter "In the Cathedral," we can see traces of K.'s recognition of the meaning of the priest's words in his resolution to dismiss his lawyer. See *Franz Kafka Today*, ed. Angel Flores and Homer Swander (Madison, Wisconsin, 1964).

limitations upon human knowledge. From the opening pages of the book it is K.'s first goal that he "become clear about his situation." Only then is useful action possible. And approximate knowledge is not enough. Or, in the words of Fräulein Montag to K., "the slightest uncertainty even in the most trifling matter is always a worry" (*T*, p. 99; *P*, p. 100) and K.'s worries, so far from being trifling, are actually a matter of life and death.

If we press the implications of phenomenological theory, we may see K.'s refusal to accept the ambivalent answer to his questions as a failure to recognize the real significance of the process of asking questions. We could say, perhaps, that K. does not perform the phenomenological reduction. It is one of Husserl's basic assertions that consciousness is *intentional*, that is, directed toward a selected object in the world. The object is not revealed until it is an object for consciousness. Then Husserl, attempting to provide a foundation for philosophy, performs the phenomenological reduction. He makes the intentional act of consciousness itself an object for consciousness; the result of this is to reveal that consciousness is the source of meaning in the world. Pierre Thévenaz, a Swiss philosopher, explains it this way:

> The primordial and essential purpose of the reduction is to bring to light this essential intentional contact between consciousness and the world, a relationship which in the natural attitude remains veiled. For Husserl, in the reduction the world remains where it is, but now one perceives that every act of knowledge in fact refers to a subject . . . as to an ultimate and primary term which is the origin, the support or foundation of its meaning.[13]

Josef K. continually flirts with the idea that man himself confers meanings on the world, much as Husserl affirms. He says to Frau Grubach, for example:

> If immediately on awakening I had got up without troubling my head about Anna's absence and had come to you without regarding anyone who tried to bar my way, I could have breakfasted in the kitchen for a change and could have got you to bring me my clothes from my room; *in short, if I had behaved sensibly, nothing further would have happened, all this would have been nipped in the bud* (*T*, p. 26; *P*, pp. 30–31; italics mine).

K. seems here to be aware that he is, by virtue of his recognition of the arrest, a collaborator in his trial. This is not, of course, to say that the trial is merely a figment of K.'s imagination; rather this points to the significance of the point of contact between consciousness and the world. The world is there; there would have been someone "[trying] to bar . . . [his] way." But, K. suggests, he had the power to focus his attention only upon the routine things of life. He could have "behaved sensibly" and thus would not have revealed the levels of human experience symbolized by the

---

[13] Pierre Thévenaz, *What Is Phenomenology?* ed. James M. Edie (Chicago, 1962), p. 47.

trial.¹⁴ This constituting power of consciousness is quite explicitly reiterated by K. during his interrogation: "It is only a trial if I recognize it as such. But for the moment I recognize it, on the grounds of compassion, as it were" (*T*, p. 51; *P*, p. 55).¹⁵ Of particular importance here is the emphasis upon meaning; K. does not assert that proceedings would not exist without his recognition. What he says is that the proceedings would not exist as his "trial" without his recognition (". . . denn es ist ja nur ein Verfahren, wenn ich es *als solches* Anerkenne"). But if K. confers meaning on the proceedings in which he is involved, why should he not solve his problems simply by refusing to recognize his trial or by manufacturing a satisfactory defense? The answer is, of course, that both solutions are impossible. Consciousness is intentional, directed toward an object, but directed toward an object which is *there*. Were the story different, K. might remain totally absorbed by daily routine. Once K. becomes conscious of the proceedings as *his trial*, however, he may deny the perception or modify it by subsequent perceptions, but he cannot simply do away with the original awareness. To the extent that his statements imply that he can rescind his recognition of the trial he is deluded or bluffing. And since consciousness intends an object in the world, it in no sense "manufactures" that toward which it is directed. If K. does not become aware of an adequate defense, no action or exercise of will can bring it into being.

By implication, K. perceives the futility of trying to rescind his recognition of the trial. He does not, however, explore the implications of this perception. His comments upon the role of his awareness in conferring meaning upon the trial are haphazard, intuitive, and delivered, as it were, in the heat of battle from the "natural standpoint." ¹⁶ They do not have the character of systematic phenomenological inquiry which places the perceived object "in brackets" and focuses attention upon the perception, upon the intentional act of consciousness. Consequently, K. continues to look for meanings and answers "out there"—he questions his wardens, the lawyer, Leni, the painter, the priest. Were he to understand the implications of his statement ("It is only a trial because I recognize it as such"), he would direct his attention toward his recognition, toward consciousness as a realm of pure being, and would accord his trial the

---

[14] It seems to me much more in keeping with Kafka's repeated concern with the hiddenness of truth to discuss this passage (as well as subsequent ones in which K. *fails* to understand things) in terms of the intentional nature of consciousness rather than in terms of bad faith, a later, Sartrian concept. Such an approach does not preclude K. H. Volkmann-Schluck's suggestion that, on one level, K. is "arrested" by consciousness itself, especially if one regards consciousness as a reflexive consciousness. For the latter idea, see "Bewußtsein und Dasein in Kafkas *Prozeß*," *Die neue Rundschau*, No. 1 (1951), 39.

[15] For a paragraph even more strikingly suggestive of the constituting power of consciousness consider the passage stricken from *P*, p. 20 and *T*, p. 16, and published in *P*, pp. 304–305 and *T*, pp. 318–319.

[16] For elaboration of this term see *Ideas*, § 30–§ 31.

bracketed position it requires as that which "essentially lacks independence" (*Ideas*, § 50). He would see that "Reality is not in itself something absolute, . . . it is, absolutely speaking, nothing at all, it has no 'absolute essence' whatever, it has the essentiality of something which in principle is *only* intentional, *only* known, consciously presented as an appearance" (*Ideas*, § 50).

From this point of view, K.'s failure to get the knowledge he desires so desperately is the result of his looking in the wrong place. We have convincing evidence of Kafka's concern with "looking in the wrong place" in a section of his diaries recorded while he was writing *Der Prozeß*. The following entry, for September 28, 1915, immediately precedes one in which Kafka refers to Josef K. by name:

> Why is it meaningless to ask questions? To complain means to put a question and wait for the answer. But questions that don't answer themselves at the very moment of their asking are never answered. No distance divides the interrogator from the one who answers him. There is no distance to overcome. Hence meaningless to ask and wait.

For K. to ask questions and wait is meaningless. The court which he questions represents (on one level) a sphere which is within, and those questions which he cannot answer—"how can any man be called guilty? We are all simply men here, one as much as the other"—are destined to remain unanswered forever. This thought is not identical with Husserl's in this sense: whereas Husserl rules out the existence of an absolute realm other than that of the Absolute Being of consciousness, Kafka does not. There may be meaningful questions about an absolute realm other than that of consciousness—but the phenomenological rules apply in the sense that testimony about that realm lies within man. Wilhelm Emrich, in *Franz Kafka*, has already provided us with a convincing and systematic explanation of Kafka's pervasive concern with the hiddenness of truth within man (*v.* esp. "Der Weg zur universellen Wahrheit," pp. 45–53). Even the metaphor of much of Kafka's prose, particularly "The Hunter Gracchus," corresponds to what Thévenaz identifies as "the distinctive signs of the phenomenological method: a method of 'showing' (*Aufweisung*), or uncovering or laying bare (*Freilegung*), of making explicit (*Auslegung*) which is meant to bring to light the forgotten being, to rediscover what lay covered or entombed." [17]

The similarity lies in this: Husserl asserts that essential truth can be discovered by an analysis of consciousness, and Kafka, analogously but far more metaphorically, affirms that essential truth must be sought hidden in the depths of man. The distinctive difference is that Husserl defines an essential truth accessible by means of the phenomenological method and

[17] Thévenaz, p. 55.

Kafka, while demonstrating that he shares many of the phenomenologist's views of cognition, remains agnostic about the finality of "essential truth" of the sort Husserl describes. Rather, for Kafka there is never a realm which man can reach which he can securely define as the realm of essential truth. Even the recognition that consciousness confers meaning on the world may be just another discovery of human responsibility in a world whose ultimate laws remain inaccessible. Perhaps, Kafka implies, this too is just another view of another table.

And it is in this sense that Josef K.'s refusal to cease asking questions is his glory as well as his failure. His questions show that he does not understand the need to quest within himself, but his questions also raise the possibility of that sphere of knowledge, of absolute *Wahrheit*, toward which it is man's glory to aspire with "raised hands" and "outspread fingers." That he does not achieve it may be shameful, but the shame may as much pertain to some order of higher *Logik* as to K. himself. K. remains in the natural standpoint, out of the realm of the phenomenological reduction, with its achievement of the essential sphere of consciousness. K.'s sphere is the realm of appearances, of the table which man circles, and thus even the last sentence of the book is irremediably ambivalent: "it seemed *as if* . . ."—"*es war, als sollte* die Scham ihn überleben."

Kafka, too, with his fundamental agnosticism about man's ability to know the truth, leaves the entire book as a symbolic structure upon which its interpreters confer meanings. We can discover in the same structure a number of meanings, and, indeed, to understand it, we must. It is clear that *Der Prozeß* may be understood in part by biographical, psychological, and philosophical approaches which draw on Kafka's *Gesammelte Werke*, as well as by careful analyses of the operation of symbol and image solely within the work itself. These varied approaches are analogous to our different perspectives on the table as we circle it. That Kafka, too, shared our experience of gathering perspectives upon the book we know from his diary entry of January 24, 1915. There, he describes reading part of *Der Prozeß* to his fiancée, Felicia Bauer, and adds: "During the reading of the doorkeeper story, greater attention and good observation. *The significance of the story dawned upon me for the first time*" (Italics mine).

Is *Der Prozeß* the chronicle of a free man defying the universe as much as man can defy it,[18] or is it the account of freely chosen bad faith,[19] or is it a record of human bondage to fears of father and marriage? [20] Without going into the critical foundations for these interpretations we may suggest that the text provides evidence that such readings may not be mutually

---

[18] Politzer, *op. cit.*

[19] René Dauvin, "*The Trial:* Its Meaning," in *Franz Kafka Today, op. cit.* See also Theodore Ziolkowski, "The Crisis of the Thirty-Year-Old in Modern Fiction," in *Comparatists at Work*, ed. Richard B. Vowles and Stephen G. Nichols, Jr. (Waltham, Mass., 1968).

[20] Charles Neider, *The Frozen Sea* (New York, 1948).

exclusive. For the reader of *Der Prozeß*, as for K., the meaning of the volume must remain ambivalent—not because the novel fails to make itself clear but because its very ambivalence is part of its clarity: the novel as a whole, like the "Legend of the Doorkeeper," stands as a symbol of man's intrinsic inability to know completely or to judge finally. The priest's melancholy quotation concerning the interpretation of the legend serves as a warning to readers and an epitome of the problems of human knowledge symbolized by the novel: "Richtiges Auffassen einer Sache und Mißverstehen der gleichen Sache schließen einander nicht vollständig aus." [21]

[21] "The right perception of any matter and a misunderstanding of the same matter do not wholly exclude each other."

Kafka's *The Trial*: The Semiotics of the Absurd

by Thomas M. Kavanagh

"Someone must have traduced Joseph K., for without having done anything wrong he was arrested one fine morning. His landlady's cook, who always brought him his breakfast at eight o'clock, failed to appear on this occasion. That had never happened before."[1] From its opening sentences Kafka's *The Trial* declares itself a departure from the normal. As a text, it elaborates itself within a universe fissured by doubt and uncertainty. A vague, unspecified "someone" becomes the subject of a hypothetical, conditional action: "must have traduced." The rhythm of the expected, the security of habit, is referred to—"His landlady's cook, who always brought him his breakfast at eight o'clock . . ."—only so that it might be more noticeably abolished: "That had never happened before."

The work's discourse inscribes itself as a moment of epistemological crisis. The story is told by a third-person objective narrator. It would be assumed, by reason of this form, that the narrator is outside the fiction, that he sees it as a whole, that his telling is at the same time a guiding and a directing. This narrative form, however, becomes itself subject to that same subversion, limitation, and cutting off which has already occurred in the story:

> Who could these men be? What were they talking about? What authority could they represent? K. lived in a country with a legal constitution, there was universal peace, all the laws were in force; who dared seize him in his own dwelling? He had always been inclined to take things easily, to believe in the worst only when the worst happened, to take no care for the morrow even when the outlook was threatening (p. 7).

From *Novel* (Spring 1972), pp. 242–245, 250–253. Copyright © 1972 by *Novel*. Reprinted by permission of the editor. Abridgments by permission of the author.

[1] Franz Kafka, *The Trial* (New York: Vintage Books, Random House, 1969), p. 3. All the quotations are from this edition (Edwin Muir's translation). Subsequent references are included in the text.

The third-person narrative voice can penetrate no further than Joseph K.'s own confused understanding of the situation. Its mode is interrogative, incomplete, and unanswered in the same way that K.'s consciousness is never totally adequate to the events he is experiencing. By reason of this narrative form, the reader's relationship to the story is, at one degree removed, exactly that of the central character's. The objectivity, the special status, the otherness of the lectorial consciousness has been called into question by the narrative form itself. To read the text is to be caught up within its epistemological crisis:

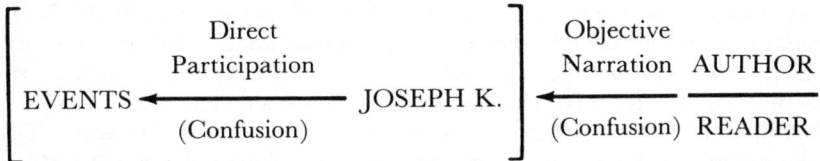

The *Trial*'s discourse is not, however, limited to that of objective third-person narration. In this opening passage, for instance, the conversation between Joseph K. and the three police agents is directly reproduced. In this atmosphere of accusation, doubt and uncertainty it is expected that the agents' words would function as a clarification and explanation. Their direct statements have, however, exactly the opposite effect. They speak only to say that they cannot speak, that they do not know, and that they cannot tell. . . . Somewhat later K. is confronted by the Inspector. He has risen one degree in the hierarchy of his accusers. Presumably the Inspector will at least be able to explain why these incomprehensible events are taking place. Given K.'s expectations, the breakdown in communication of meaning takes place even more brutally:

> "These gentlemen here and myself have no standing whatever in this affair of yours, indeed we know hardly anything about it. . . . I can't even confirm that you are charged with an offense, or rather I don't know whether you are . . . (p. 16).

To move up in the hierarchy is to become confused, to be told less, to be made even more painfully aware of the epistemological hiatus on which the entire sequence of events is based. Direct discourse becomes anti-function: telling nothing, it insists that all further inquiry be renounced.

The reassuring, almost conniving, mimesis of a Flaubert or a Dickens has given way; but it does not give way in favor of some other discourse such as that of an Aragon or a Breton. The universe of *The Trial* is a subversive universe. Language appears capable of representing what is—a tenement is a tenement, its attic is an attic—but at the very same time this representation is undermined from within.

As readers we intuitively sense these characteristics of the Kafkaesque world. As critics, however, we must concern ourselves with *The Trial* as a text: the unnamed city, its law courts, and Joseph K. "exist" only in so far as they are conjured up by a specific succession of verbal signs. The reader must somehow attempt to understand *how these words function* rather than *what it is they might mean*. The difficulty comes in choosing that critical discourse, that metaphor, which is most adequate to the text in question. The critic is confronted with a romanesque syntagme: a discourse which, when he makes attempts at understanding, proves to be extensive, discontinuous and unorganized. His task is not to abolish this discontinuity, to substitute his organized, unilinear discourse for that of the text; but rather to choose a perspective, a point of view. His particular choice is not meant to imply that all other choices are somehow invalid or distorting. The criterion for one's choices must, as Roland Barthes has pointed out,[2] be not their validity (*either* true *or* false) but rather their coherency (*more* explanatory, illuminating, etc. or *less* so in relation to the text). The metaphors that have been most commonly used for an analysis of Kafka's novels have been drawn from the discourse of psychoanalysis. Paranoia and schizophrenia (in different proportions and with various refinements) have been proposed as that which "explains" both the novels and their creator. *Opera auctoris speculum* has been the premise behind a critical journey parting from the agonies of Joseph K. in order to arrive at their source in the tribulations of the young and not-so-young Kafka seeking justification before his father.

As legitimate and coherent as such a perspective might be, it abstracts itself completely from the problem of how *The Trial* functions as a text; how it is able to communicate those impressions we have summarily described. Therefore, assuming that this text, before it can be a "case study" or a "vision of the world," is a chain of words arrayed in a unique fashion, I have chosen my critical metaphor from the discourse of semiotics: the relationship between code and message.

These are mutually defining terms: a given enunciation does not exist as a message until it is understood in terms of a particular code; this code itself can not, however, be seen as operative until a sufficient number of messages have been analyzed and the pertinent semantic axes isolated. As a semiotic concept this relationship parallels that of its specifically linguistic variation: code is to message as *langue* is to *parole*. This structure governs every area where meaning is able to exist. The length of one's hair, the clothes he wears, the words he uses: all these "facts" become messages when they are perceived in terms of the pertinent social codes. Once these codes have been learned, the speaker is able both to give out his own messages and to interpret those of others. I am of my world to the extent that I know and can manipulate its codes.

[2] Roland Barthes, *Critique et vérité* (Paris: Editions du Seuil, 1966).

The universe of *The Trial* has been referred to as absurd, as one fallen prey to an epistemological crisis. This crisis is nothing other than the absence of a code adequate to the various messages being emitted. To perceive a code is to accomplish an act of integration. It is then to the extent that one is aware of the pertinent semantic axes that he can detect meaning where before there was none. Without the code there is only a series of monolithic facts which might be experienced and reflected upon, but which can in no way be reduced and explained as the manifestation of a series of defined principles. It is through the mediation of the code that we see the present as both the result of a past and the indication of a future.

"One fine morning" Joseph K. awakens to find his world invaded by a series of discordant messages. These messages not only call into question the codes to which he is accustomed; but, in subverting their validity, they point to—yet stubbornly refuse to reveal—another more extensive code of which he is completely ignorant. Comfort, the adequacy of self to situation, is gone. With it goes both his power to understand what is said and to say what he wishes. K.'s goal is no longer that of expression and manipulation, but that of simple comprehension. The adventure of Joseph K. is an adventure of the mind, the adventure of a semiologist in spite of himself. It is the hope of penetrating the code, of restoring order and meaning to his disintegrating world that most characterizes Kafkaesque man.

Confronted with his warders, Joseph K. "wanted in some way to enter into the thoughts of the warders and twist them to his own advantage or else try to acclimatize himself to them" (p. 10). Man's plight becomes that of understanding codes, of separating and putting together once again all the pieces with the hope that some logic will declare itself, that some meaning will be unveiled, that the present will become part of an understandable temporal process having its roots in the past and its implications for the future. In desperation man imparts to every and any collection of possible differences the status of a sign: because nothing is significant, everything becomes significant. One of the accused tells K.:

> ... people are too tired and distracted to think and so they take refuge in superstition. I'm as bad as anyone myself. And one of the superstitions is that you're supposed to tell from a man's face, especially the line of his lips, how his case is going to turn out (p. 217).

. . .

The Code As Absence

To defend oneself before the law is to accept the promulgated *corpus juris* as the code effectively governing the interpretation of that particular message which is the challenged action. To defend oneself is to formulate an interpretation: a comparison of the crime as message with the dictates of the penal code as structure. It is in terms of this code that the message will be assigned a univocal meaning: innocent or guilty. As a lawyer Huld is expected to know the penal code, the code directly regulating *The Trial*'s universe. K. learns, however, that the *corpus juris* lacks that property most essential to the proper functioning of a code: the ability to eliminate internal contradiction. Even Huld's explanation of the importance of the first plea reveals the many layers of contradiction internal to the penal code:

> ... He had started on K.'s case at once, of course, and the first plea was almost ready for presentation. That was very important, for the first impression made by the Defense often determined the whole course of the subsequent proceedings.... But unluckily even that was not quite true in most cases, the first plea was often mislaid or lost altogether and, even if it were kept intact till the end, was hardly even read (pp. 143-144).

The only functioning code is arbitrary. The final judgment depends entirely upon the whim of the Examining Magistrate. With no pretense of objectivity, the only way of influencing the decision is through one's "connections." ... But even connections are meaningless: the case can at any moment be transferred to another, totally inaccessible court where all influence is impossible.

Huld, the lawyer, is never shaken by the "new" precisely because the "new" is indistinguishable from the "old." To realize that all decisions are arbitrarily handed down implies the absence of any consistency against which the new, the inconsistent, might then define itself.

At one point in K.'s epistemological odyssey the text as message adopts all the characteristics of a direct exposition of its interpretive code. Spending a morning in the deserted cathedral, Joseph K. comes upon a lone priest who insists on telling him the story of the man come before the Law. This story appears to be a clarification, a segment of the text in which indirection is temporarily put aside in favor of an immediate (if metaphoric) exposition of the work's meaning. All the signs are right. The story is told by a priest: an individual serving as a link between man and some higher power. The story itself has all the marks of a parable: barely more than two pages in length, its characters and situations are reduced to the minimal archetype of seeker and obstacle; the universal—and universalizing—tense is that of the present; the sequence is reduced to the skeletal triad of arrival, death, and a vast but undifferentiated time of waiting. The entire exposition, the parable as such, serves to concentrate the listener's attention on the supposed meaning in the guardian's response to the seeker's final question: "No one but you could gain admittance through that door, since that door was intended only for you. I am now going to shut it" (p. 269).

The code governing the Kafkaesque universe seems at last to be manifesting itself. But what is the meaning; what is the code? K. himself remains confused. The priest, as though responding to K.'s perplexity, adopts a form of discourse which becomes "meta-textual." He himself will provide an interpretation of his parable.

The most important characteristic of this interpretation is its resolute *multiplicity*. The parable itself becomes a limited set of semes from which an infinite number of possible subsets can be successively generated. The guardian is first seen as a "precisian with a stern regard for duty." . . . This same guardian is then presented as being simple-minded and rather conceited. . . . Finally, with a complete reversal, he is depicted as a friendly and pitying man. . . .

These interpretations, because of their circular, self-justifying relation to the text, could continue indefinitely. The priest is not unaware of the problem he is raising. He explicitly states that commentary, the attempt to determine meaning, is an act of despair:

> "Don't misunderstand me," said the priest, "I am only showing you the various opinions concerning that point. You must not pay too much attention to them. The scriptures are unalterable and the comments often enough merely express the commentator's despair" (p. 272).

The priest's parable and its contradictory interpretations . . . function as a microcosm revealing that same impossibility characterizing the work as a whole: the impossibility of interpretation.

The "message" of both parable and text is that there is no message, that there is no universal code in terms of which all is able to "mean," to become one, to become subject to the dictates of the apparently logical. Kafkaesque man remains forever separated from the illumination of the Law, the illumination of the code.

Code-Message and the Literary Work

The code-message relationship seems almost to impose itself in the analysis of the literary work. Language itself, as a symbolic system, demands the prior knowledge of a particular code (the English or German language, for instance). It is perhaps for this reason that literature's particular use of language has often been presented as the activation of secondary code or codes which rearray the lexemes of the original message according to a new unity, a new *gestalt*, a new meaning. Orwell's *Animal Farm* would, for instance, according to the primary code of the English language, be a message dealing with the rather strange adventures of a group of animals endowed with human faculties. This same text seems, however, to demand a further perception of itself in terms of a second code which might be called the general political situation of the 1930s or, in less neutral terms, the liberal ideology of the pre-war western democracies. According to this view a text's literary status would refer to its being inexhaustible in terms of any single code, but opting instead for a resolutely polysemantic status of many codes operating upon many messages.

But what is, in fact, the function of these supposedly secondary codes? No matter how numerous we might make them, they are essentially a means of abolishing the text as a text. Their enumeration is a way of taking what has declared itself as *other than* an immediately signifying use of language and treating it as if it were only the slightly more occult kernel of some recuperating meaning.

Our . . . analysis of *The Trial* has shown it to be constructed as the systematic refusal of all access to any such secondary codes. The text is there. It presents itself as message, but for all its tension, for all its straining, it unveils no code, it conveys no univocal meaning. It speaks only of its own incompleteness, of its own inviolability. Disguised as message, it reveals only the form of its disguise.

The literary word is the fully activated word, the word manifesting the *movement* of language as act rather than the *death* of language as a finished, meaningful resumé of some intention. The text remains, unendingly, that inevitable movement from signifier to signifier which is the basis of all language. Every signified meaning which might be drawn from this movement is itself subverted by, caught up in, and redefined in terms of a choreography which knows no end, which remains forever alien to that cut-off of meaning which would freeze the dance into some calcified pose of meaning. What is distinctive to the literary is not a code, or any series of codes. It is instead that movement of an only apparent message forever changing, forever soliciting meanings, and forever redefining itself.

Joseph K. becomes the subject of a truly literary discourse at that moment when his self-assured perception of the codes governing his world is shaken and destroyed. It is as the *inexplicable* breaks in upon his world that we, as readers, begin to follow the unfolding of his odyssey.

Likewise, it is only when K.'s assurance as to the meaning of his acts is subverted that he himself becomes capable of assuming the function of the "writer":

> He had often considered whether it would not be better to draw up a written defense and hand it in to the Court. In this defense he would give a short account of his life, and when he came to an event of any importance explain for what reasons he had acted as he did, intimate whether he approved or condemned his way of action in retrospect, and adduce grounds for the condemnation or approval (p. 142).

In desperation K. attempts to emit a message (that of his entire life) so complete in its scope and explanations that it necessarily justify him before the Court's impenetrable code. This desperation, this impossibility, makes of K.'s autobiography, like his biography, an act of language founded upon an absence, an irretrievable alienation from all meaning.

Man Guilty

by Erich Heller

... Even if it were possible to suppress those unsophisticated questions —what is the Law, what is the guilt?—for short spells of shock and intense captivation, it would be unfeasible in the long run, and it is the long run that accounts for the decisive flaw of *The Trial*. There is a certain tiresomeness in those ever-repeated descriptions of the Court's enormously complicated structure with its higher judges never visible or reachable; in the assertions, made again and again, of the infallibility of the Court's involvements so that there is always guilt where it becomes active ("Once it has brought a charge against someone, the Court can never be dislodged from that conviction," we learn from Titorelli, among others); in the reiterated characterizations of the accessible seats of justice and all its agencies as dirty, corrupt, oppressive, unaired, and fostering sexual exploitation.

All this, however, is as nothing compared to the structural imbalance which in the end threatens to bring down the building: the ever-present difficulty, that is, of reconciling the glorious presence and unquestioned validity of the invisible Law with the inglorious existence and dubious character of its mundane executants; or the radiance that pours forth from the interior of the truth (perceived, characteristically, only by the country man grown blind with age) with the fleas in the fur coats of its guardians; or the beauty which the Law appears to bestow upon those who are indicted in its name ("The accused are all beautiful," says the Lawyer, explaining why his maid Leni is so much attracted to K.) with the terrible fate it holds in store for them. Not that it would be hard to make one's peace with the contrast between the impurity of the creature and the pure light that is the essence of the Creator: Jews and Christians have learned this much in school. But in Kafka's novels, certainly in *The Trial*, original sin is as it were too sinful by half, and yet must—confusingly—be thought of as the richest source of virtue.

It is not easy to apply the story of the Fall to the case of Joseph K.,

---

"Man Guilty" [editor's title], from *Franz Kafka*, by Erich Heller, pp. 82–90, 97. Copyright © 1974 by Erich Heller. Reprinted by permission of The Viking Press, Inc.

although certainly it has some bearing. Kafka was convinced that he understood "the Fall of Man better than anyone"; but if he intended to make *The Trial* into an allegory of original sin, he certainly did not succeed and indeed was bound to fail, if for no other reason than because the *universality* of the Biblical disaster cannot be represented through the very particular destiny of one person, an ordinary person at that, or even of many persons, in contrast to the rest of mankind.[1] Or is the reader to believe that the Manufacturer or the Assistant Director of K.'s Bank—to name only two characters from the novel—is immune from the malady caused by the apple, although they may never have breakfasted on apples, as K. does on the morning of his arrest? His sin must be a particular one, even if it is rooted in the universal one; must be a sin not shared by the Manufacturer or Assistant Manager; and, to deserve the sentence of death, must be more substantial than the crumbs of guilt the moral reader may pick up in the course of the novel—K.'s loveless sexuality, his indifference to his mother, or his lack of courage in not interfering with the whipping of the warders (in a scene, moreover, that is too dreamlike for moral judgments to rush in).

If there is any explanation for Kafka's ruinous compulsion to insist at the same time and in the same work upon the ultimately incompatible, the goodness of the Law and the evil of its application, it may be found in the pathology of his spiritual imagination, now quasi-Manichaean and now again drawn toward an emphatic and emphatically worldly yea-saying. "There is nothing but a spiritual world," he wrote in his "Reflections on Sin, Suffering, Hope, and the True Way," "and what we call the world of the senses, is the Evil in the spiritual world." Therefore any attempt to translate the spiritual into the tangibly concrete—and what else is the business of art or that of the worldly administering of Justice?—is with him in constant danger of yielding nothing but evil. Let the Law shine in transcendent brightness behind the last gate of reality; its secular execution is, with inexorable logic, entrusted to "the scoundrels of the

---

[1] The nineteenth-century German dramatist Friedrich Hebbel tried to solve a similar problem by choosing as his hero or heroine a person equipped with quite extraordinary gifts, thus symbolically creating *the* individual because this *exceptional* individual is more of an individual than others: Agnes Bernauer through her surpassing beauty, Siegfried through his exceptional strength. But this is not what Kafka does with Joseph K. A passage in the "Letter to His Father" comes close, in personal and domestic terms, to stating, if not explaining, the relationship between Joseph K., the Law, and the rest of the world: "The world was for me divided into three parts: one in which I lived under laws which had been invented only for me and which I could, I did not know why, never completely comply with; then a second world, which was infinitely remote from mine, in which you lived, concerned with government, with the issuing of orders, and with the annoyance about their not being obeyed; and finally a third world where everybody else lived happily and free from orders and from having to obey." Although this is strikingly relevant to *The Trial*, it also shows the distance between a personal situation and its literary "mythological" transformation.

Court's lower order," as Kafka puts it in the chapter "The Whipper." To turn to them in the expectation of justice is to hope for consolation from fleas; and as in the physical domain all individual life ends in death, so the stabbing in the quarry awaits him who is guilty of living in the world. For, as another Manichaean saying of Kafka's—in the same series of aphorisms—will have it: "The fact that there is nothing but a spiritual world deprives us of hope and gives us certainty." We need not ask what certainty. It is, in this "unreal" world, abrupt and deadly, even if the spirit is bound "hopelessly" to survive in the "only real" world.

Guilty of living? Of living in the world? If Kafka's imagination had simply been received into the Manichaean heresy, and if it had come to rest with the assurance that, as he put it in that sequence of "Reflections," "there can be knowledge of the diabolical but no belief in it, for there is nothing more diabolical than what exists," we would no longer have to ask why, in contrast to the luminosity of the invisible and unreachable Law, its doorkeepers are so dismal, its judges so mischievous, and its executioners so devilish. The unhappy but simple answer would be: because they exist. Kafka's terrible observation about knowledge, belief, and evil will have it that the whole world of the senses, the world "as we know it," is so perfect a realization of the diabolical as to leave no room for *believing* in evil; this is so because the proper object of *belief* is not the empirical but the transcendental world, the world not of the senses but of the spirit. The empirical world—and that, according to the aphorism, means Evil—is the province of *knowledge*. Thus it makes good sense for someone to say, "I believe in God," but it makes no sense (except, in English, a vaguely idiomatic one) to believe in doorknobs, influenza, or—the diabolical. If, therefore, it would be correct to assume that for Kafka the officials of the Court are, because they act in the world, *necessarily* corrupt, his would be a frightening but logically consistent world. Yet it is not. For Kafka means K.—and meant himself—to be guilty at the same time of an insufficiency in living *here and now*, of a lack of *faith in life*, the very life that is nonetheless seen as "the Evil in the spiritual world," indeed as the devil itself.

Never before has an artist so compulsively tried to hold simultaneously and weld together in works of art such irreconcilably contrary beliefs. Kafka, it seems, did exactly this in *The Trial*, and this is why the novel confronts the reader and interpreter not so much with difficulties as with inescapable defeat. For he who denied the reality of any world but that of the spirit, and who saw in life as it is lived the incarnation of the devil, *also* said that "in the struggle between yourself and the world you must take the side of the world"—"One must not cheat anyone, not even the world, of its victory"—and said it immediately before he reduced the world of the senses to nothing but "the Evil in the spiritual world." And entering the sphere in which *The Trial* is domiciled, we hear him say (a little later in the same collection of aphorisms) that we are "sinful not only because we have eaten of the Tree of Knowledge, but also because we have not yet eaten of the Tree of Life. The state in which we are is sinful, irrespective of guilt." We have lost Paradise by our sinfully being cast into the world, but then we have sinned once more, this time against the world, by not living in it courageously and abundantly. For Kafka's Tree of Life is certainly not the other tree in Eden that the Lord felt he had to protect from so ambitious a creature as man, intent upon himself becoming God, but is a tree that grows in the fields cultivated by Adam and Eve in the sweat of their brows.

"Marrying, founding a family, accepting all the children that come, supporting them in this insecure world and even guiding them a little is, I am convinced, the utmost a human being can succeed in doing at all," Kafka wrote in the "Letter to His Father," accusing his parent of having stood between him and this good life. Instead of leading this good life, he became, as we have heard him say, "literature": "I . . . am made of literature, I am nothing else and cannot be anything else." Where is now the spiritual world with its claim to being the only true reality—*if* indeed Kafka ever found his spiritual reality in his art? Certainly, we know that at times he bitterly lamented the absence of any such reality from his living, that, as he said to Max Brod in the long letter of July 1922, he remained clay because he did not use the spark for lighting a fire but merely for illuminating his deadness, that is, for making literature.

Yet in another letter to Felice (March 17–18, 1913) he had equated being fully alive with having the inspiration to write. But then again he could not marry her—"everything in me revolted against it," he wrote in his diary (March 9, 1914)—because "marriage would have endangered my literary work." Elsewhere, in the letter to Brod, he again condemns literary work, not because it is bad but because it is evil. He is "sustained" by it, yet the life thus sustained is dedicated to serving "the devil." But at another time, among the fragments of *Wedding Preparations*, this mingling with the powers of darkness, his writing, appears to him as "a form of prayer"; and recording in his diary the commotion ensuing upon Austria's mobilization in the summer of 1914, he vows that he must at all costs continue writing, for this is *his* "struggle for self-preservation." The circle could not be more vicious. It is a paranoid situation that, were it not for his literary powers of resistance, would probably have developed into insanity.

Kafka knew this himself. To Brod he spoke of the terrible enslavement of the writer by his writing table: "He must never move away from it, must hold onto it with all his might, if he does not want to fall into madness." This, even today, is not likely to be true of many writers and would have been received as a crazy notion by most before the nineteenth century, for then, as Baudelaire put it with a grand and imprecise gesture, the poetic consciousness was an inexhaustible source of delights; afterward, he believed, it became "an inexhaustible arsenal of torture instruments." ²

This reads as if anachronistically Baudelaire had had Kafka in mind; certainly the product of Kafka's servitude at the writing desk shows symptoms of the madness which the writing kept from breaking out in real life: the terrible logic of the absurd which is characteristic of paranoia as well as of Kafka's inventions, the nightmares that the insomniac Kafka would have suffered had he found sleep. As it was, he dreamed them during his nocturnal writing hours and narrated them in that wakefully sober and controlled prose that is so rare in German.

There can be no other novel so thoroughly pervaded by the sense of nightmare and paranoia as *The Trial*. "They [innocuous fellow lodgers in the boardinghouse] had perhaps been standing there all the time, they scrupulously avoided all appearance of having been observing him, they talked in low voices, following K.'s movements only with the abstracted gaze one has for people passing when one is deep in conversation. All the same, their glances weighed heavily upon K., and he made what haste he could to his room, keeping close against the wall." There is a plethora of such scenes in the novel: faces in windows across the street looking with intense curiosity into K.'s room; ears, real or imagined, pressed against doors; figures suddenly discovered standing and watching in the shadow of gateways; eyes peering through keyholes; defense lawyers who—"a possibility not to be excluded"—may secretly work for the defendant's accusers; rooms that had always been presumed to be quite ordinary and that, upon inspection, reveal themselves as torture chambers. In the last instance, a man called Franz is being whipped, and K., detecting the horror, guiltily considers taking Franz's place. K. substituting for Franz: nobody initiated into Kafka's way with names will believe that Franz, one of the two warders of the Court who is now to be punished for having conducted himself reprehensibly when he arrested K., bears his author's name without purpose. It is the schizophrenia within, the laceration of identity, that outwardly becomes two persons, christened Franz and K., and thereby exorcised, just as the whole trial seems to be the perfect protective scheme designed by a paranoiac imagination. At every point it reflects the patient's contempt for the persecuting powers and at the same time his eagerness inwardly to bow to their authority; his persistent refusal to acknowledge any guilt on his part ("he admits that he doesn't know the Law and yet he claims he's innocent," Franz exclaims in the scene of the arrest in which K. finds himself incomprehensibly "decoyed into an exchange of speaking looks" with Franz); and, disastrously intermixed with this, his straining to imprison himself more and more in the cell of an unknown offense.

. . .

---

² Charles Baudelaire, *Oeuvres complètes*, Collection de la Pléiade (Paris, 1954, 1969), p. 519.

He who transcended psychology also transcended the literary form of the novel. At Kafka's hands novels were bound to remain fragmentary. Bertolt Brecht proved to be a perspicacious critic when he spoke to Walter Benjamin of Kafka's ultimate failure as a novelist.[3] He failed, Brecht said, because he was meant to be what Confucius was: he had the disposition and gift of a great teacher, but, as there was for Kafka no society to teach or prophetically to inspire, his Confucian parables illegitimately became "literature," "mere" literature. ("If I were a Chinese . . ." Kafka once wrote to Felice [May 1916], and added, "Indeed I am a Chinese.") The prophetic parables grew into "art," even into abortive novels, and thus lost their parabolic consistency and seriousness. "They were never quite transparent," said Brecht. This is also the reason why the apparent precision of Kafka's style is so deceptive: it is the precision of an exact dream confusingly dreamt in a place between prophecy and art.

It remains the great virtue of Kafka's failure that he presents guilt as an *Urphänomen*, an irreducible phenomenon. Within the world of *The Trial* guilt has no legal content or sufficient psychological cause. It is, for Kafka, part of the anatomy of the soul, just as is the impossible search of the restlessly homeless mind in *The Castle*.

[3] Walter Benjamin, *Versuche über Brecht* (Frankfurt am Main, 1966), pp. 119 ff.

The Question of the Law, the Question of Writing

by Stanley Corngold

In the middle of the great penultimate chapter of *The Trial*, the priest who is to be revealed as the prison chaplain reproves Josef K. "You cast about too much for outside help," he declares, "especially from women." Josef K. will not accept this rebuke. He sets about defending the influence of women accomplices in his case. "If I could move some women I know to join forces in working for me, I couldn't help winning through. Especially before this Court, which consists almost entirely of petticoat-hunters." Something the priest does next warns Josef K. that the priest is furious with him: K.'s mood is caught by the growing oppressiveness of the scene, the murkiness of the air: "Black night had set in." Everything in the moment suggests K. at the point of greatest estrangement from his own predicament. And in his next words the reason for this estrangement comes to light. "It may be," says Josef K. audaciously to the priest, "that you do not know the nature of the Court you are serving." In the silence which follows, K. adds weakly, "These are only my personal experiences." An instant later the priest shrieks from his pulpit: "Can't you see one pace before you?" The narrator comments: "It was an angry cry, but at the same time sounded like the unwary shriek of one who sees another fall and is startled out of his senses."

The mood of this moment conveys as much as any other moment in *The Trial* the quality of an authentic revelation. Josef K. has in principle asserted that, unlike the priest, he *knows* the nature of the Court and that he knows it on the basis of personal experiences. The priest's response is to indict this position of sheer, mad blindness, of error and delusion so heavy as almost literally to drag the speaker down to his fall.

This moment comes well prepared. From the outset the novel conceives Josef K.'s trial by the court as the issue of his acknowledging the question of its nature and authority. "What authority, he asks of the men who come to arrest him, "could they represent?" But K.'s summing-up in the cathedral—a meager insight based on a persistent evasion of his situation —concludes a year-long refusal to penetrate the question. The character of this refusal is clarified further by the account of his state of mind which immediately precedes and follows this moment.

At the beginning of his exchange with the chaplain, K. declares what he has declared before: "I am not guilty; . . . it is a mistake." This is a position which Josef K. can maintain only in defiance of the Court. "You are held to be guilty," the priest has said—for the Court is drawn by the guilt of those it arrests. Josef K. can properly maintain his innocence vis-à-vis the law of the Court only in the conviction that the Court has erred in arresting him at all. But what does K. know of the nature of the Court which could allow for a mistake of this order? We have seen that he will try to authorize his judgment of the (derelict) character of the Court by an appeal to his own experiences. But the chaplain has already pre-empted this argument, for, to Josef K.'s claim of innocence on the grounds that no one man is any more guilty than another, the priest retorts: "That is true, but that is how all guilty men talk." This is to say that the perception into the nature of the court which accuses it of dereliction cannot be well founded on "personal experiences," since the personal experiences of the guilty are distorted, circumscribed, broken-off according to the character of their guilt. Josef K. is inculpated by his very impatience to find himself innocent; it prevents him from pondering faithfully the essential question: What, apart from the urgency of my need to find myself innocent, is the nature and authority of the law? And since in this trial "the proceedings . . . gradually merge into the verdict," it is impossible that Josef K. can produce a saving insight. He will not in all seriousness keep open the possibility of his guilt; he will not follow the track of an equivocation which must affirm—as the claim of innocence must deny—an "arrest," the sense of which is to be seized by the question of the nature and authority of the law. We recall again the chaplain's shriek of dismay at K.'s madness in asserting a knowledge of the Court based on the kind of experience of the Court he has so far had. It is entirely consistent with K.'s character that he then responds to the priest's outrage with a plan to use the priest to help him "circumvent his case, break away from it altogether, [find] a mode of living completely outside the jurisdiction of the Court."

The attitude which Kafka solicits and which Josef K. fails to provide is one of openness to the possibility of guilt. This amounts to the self's assuming the burden of an arrest or captivation by an unknown, "invisible" authority. It is to ask the question of the meaning of the law with all possible seriousness, a devotion which turns one's whole life into a question. We want to ask now, what intensity of concern urges Kafka to articulate this theme?

Undoubtedly there is a good deal of plausibility to the familiar argument that sees Kafka *qua* ontologist, as posing in the manner of Heidegger in *Sein und Zeit* the question of the meaning of Being in terms of an analysis of the finite, culpable, evasive, individual human *Dasein*. Kafka, however, does not finally encourage us to consider himself a philosopher. He wrote in 1912:

> When it became clear in my organism that writing was the most productive direction for my being to take, everything rushed in that direction and left empty all those abilities which were directed toward the joys of sex, eating, drinking, [and] philosophical reflection. . . .

When one speaks of the concern which indeed held Kafka on trial and in thrall throughout his life, it becomes necessary to speak of writing. It is impossible to overestimate the seriousness with which Kafka felt the moral claim of the being he called *Schriftstellersein* ("being literature")—the force which laid on him an inquiry into the nature of writing and of his trial by writing. Now the relation of the categories of the law, of being on trial, and of culpability to literature has often been raised à propos of *The Trial*, but in the particular perspective of Kafka's troubled relation with his fiancée Felice Bauer. Stated baldly, Kafka puts a persona of himself on trial for having decided between literature and marriage. In a letter to Felice written only weeks after he had begun composing *The Trial*, Kafka wrote:

> You see, you were not only the greatest friend but at the same time also the greatest enemy of my writing, at least seen from the standpoint of my work, and therefore, as in its core it loved you beyond all limits, in its self-preservation it had to fight you off with all its might.

The force of writing for him is that of a literally constitutive function of his identity. "My way of life," he wrote, "is oriented solely toward writing." "Writing is the sole inner possibility of my existence." "Writing is my good nature." To marry would be to compromise his purity, to scatter his intensity. He broke off his engagement with Felice—but in the bachelorhood that ensued he could not write either.

He was consumed, he wrote in 1914, by the one thought. Breaking with Felice, he was guilty perhaps of having abused the woman he loved. Without exculpation he could not live on as a writer. Literature appears as the one possible agency of his exculpation; and he is forced to a renewed inquiry into the nature of the justifying authority—his art—at the same time that literature remains hidden, absconded. What are the implications of the fact that it will not come? How can he know whether he is guilty or innocent and toward whom? His broken engagement exacerbates the question of the authority of literature—an authority possibly dubious in itself or one toward which he is guilty of neglect. But it does not raise the question for the first time or in its most rigorous form.

Readers of Kafka's diaries and letters will appreciate the complexity of Kafka's relation to literature: The rich thematic structures of *The Trial* persist independently of Kafka's relation to his fiancée. A letter to Max

Brod written at the end of Kafka's life describes "writing as aiming toward nothing other than the salvation or damnation of [my] own soul"; but in a stunning phrase written when Kafka was twenty, he states: "God does not want me to write—I, however, I must." These propositions constitute a space outside of God's order, in which safety is gained by taking obscure, even "devilish," risks—a proving ground for justification according to a law unknown or of one's own devising. The connection between Kafka the writer and the enthralling law of writing explicitly parallels that between Josef K. and the law in a diary entry for 1910: "How shall I excuse the fact that I have not yet written anything today? In no way (*mit nichts*). . . . I have continually an invocation in my ear: 'If you would come, invisible court!'" Between 1910 and 1913 the claim of the court has struck definitively. In 1913 Kafka described himself to Felice as one "chained with invisible chains to an invisible literature, who cries aloud when someone comes near, because his chains, he asserts, are being fingered." (One thinks of the accused gentleman in the law offices who screams when Josef K. touches his arm "quite loosely"; the usher's comment is: "Most of these accused men are so sensitive.")

The period just before the writing of *The Trial*—we've noted—was unusually full of expressions of despair at Kafka's shortcomings vis-à-vis his writing. Kafka was thirty on June 3, 1913; on November 18, 1913, he wrote: "In the meantime how much doubt about my writing have I had," and on March 9, 1914: "For a whole year I have written nothing." Kafka's thirtieth year, like Josef K.'s, stood in a steadily disintegrating relation to the law, at the same time that the law required a more and more total devotion. Kafka perceives that his own powers are too fragile: The point is made with dreadful intensity in the diary entry of August 6, 1914, which very nearly coincides with the onset of the composition of *The Trial*:

> What will be my fate as a writer is very simple. My talent for portraying my dreamlike inner life has thrust all other matters into the background; my life has dwindled dreadfully, nor will it cease to dwindle. Nothing else will ever satisfy me. But the strength I can muster for that portrayal is not to be counted upon: perhaps it has already vanished forever, perhaps it will come back to me again. . . . Thus I waver, continually fly to the summit of the mountain, but then fall back in a moment. . . . But I waver on the heights; it is not death, alas, but the eternal torments of dying.

Literature, like the court, figures as the grim agency requiring the sacrifice not only of sexual love but of all of life itself.

In this perspective Kafka's relation to writing is intrinsically guilty; as long as he lives he cannot be equal to his fate. He is guilty toward writing in other ways which are impossible to specify unequivocally, but whose locus can be traced. His texts modulate the notion of guilt in terms of any writing which he could produce; writing bent on self-justification; writing as a defense against or celebration of the world; writing that goes badly; and not writing at all. If a single formulation should serve, it is this:

> Writing means indeed to open oneself to an excessive degree; the most extreme openness of heart and devotion in which a human being in human relations believes that he is already losing himself and thus from which—as long as he has not lost his senses—he will always shrink back . . . —this openness of heart and devotion does not by far suffice for writing.

Yet in 1912 Kafka could say of the quality of his devotion:

> I have never been someone who carried something through at all costs. . . . What I've written was written in a warm bath. I have not experienced the eternal hell of the real writer.

Here Kafka registers in himself what he will register in Josef K.: faintheartedness in the question of the authority of the law. In tracing Josef K.'s bad faith, he literally enacts his identity as one in thrall to the law. But this process occurs through a significant distortion.

In *The Trial* Josef K., unlike the author, refuses to write a line in his own defense; the act of writing is detached from him, displaced onto the opposing principle, and devalued, for writing appears as an indecipherable or obscene screed, another shabby appurtenance of the Court. There is a second significant difference. Josef K.—who is guilty in the sense of having been arrested and in the sense of having evaded the question of the authority of the law—never asserts a guilty conscience. As a persona of Kafka, K. can be conceived as conscienceless because of his very rejection and devaluation of writing. But the terms of conscience and writing are precisely constitutive of Kafka. With an acute sense of guilt Kafka writes and judges his own productions and himself as author. It is because he abides and finally makes generative a sense of despair that he is able, unlike Josef K., to evoke in this novel the pure virtual form of an authentic relation to the law.

Kafka's Principal Works and His Recorded Private Reading

Kafka's writings are often interpreted in terms of the claustrophobia of his familial and social situation. As a mild antidote to this approach, the following schema focuses on the fact, to which Kafka is no exception, that a principal source of all literature is the fruitful confrontation with other texts. References made by Kafka to significant writers, not merely in passing, are listed here, as attested by three basic sources: the *Diaries* (D), the standard edition of *Letters* (L), and the *Letters to Felice* (LF). Obviously editorial selectivity is involved; and obviously, too, suggestive patterns in the listings, for example, Kafka's references to Dostoevsky throughout the period of *The Trial* (July–December, 1914) should not lead to premature conclusions about "influence." All the table does is to indicate the general literary context Kafka created for himself.

	WORKS	RECORD OF READING
1904	"Description of a Struggle"	Jan.: Gustave Flaubert (L); Goethe: *Werther* (L).
1904–1912	Prose pieces finally collected in *Meditation* (1915)	Jan. 27: Friedrich Hebbel: *Diaries* (L); Thomas Mann: "Tonio Kröger" (L).
1907	"Wedding Preparations in the Country"	Sept. Jens Peter Jacobsen: *Niels Lyhne* (L).
1908		May: Robert Walser (L).
1909		April: Knut Hamsun (L).
1910		Nov. 7: Hebbel (D); Dec. 19: Goethe: *Diaries* (D); Dec. 27: Leo Tolstoy: "The Kreutzer Sonata" (D).
1911	*America* (until winter 1912)	Jan. 14, Sept. 26: Hamsun (D). Jan. 27: Heinrich von Kleist (L); Feb. 20, Nov. 23: Kleist (D); Aug. 20: Charles Dickens (D); Oct. 1, Dec. 26: Goethe (D); Oct. 26: George Bernard Shaw (D); Oct. 30: *Die Aktion* (D); Dec. 23: Franz Werfel (D).

1912	Sept. 22-23: "The Judgment" Nov.: "The Metamorphosis"	Feb. 4: Frank Wedekind: *Erdgeist* (D); Feb. 4, 5, 8, March 3, 17, Aug. 15: Goethe (D); March 16, June 6, July 15, 20: Flaubert (D); March 28, Aug. 9: Franz Grillparzer (D); July 10: Kleist (L), Sigmund Freud (D); Sept. 23: Freud, Werfel (D); Nov. 15, Dec. 4: Flaubert: *L'Education Sentimentale* (LF); Nov. 21, Dec. 9: August Strindberg (LF); Dec. 12: Werfel: *Der Weltfreund* (LF).
1913		Jan. 16: Flaubert (LF); Jan. 19: Martin Buber (LF); Jan. 27, 28: Hebbel: Letters (LF); Feb. 1: Werfel (LF); Feb. 9: Kleist (LF); March 13: Goethe: *Werther*, Flaubert (LF); July 21: Flaubert, Grillparzer, Fyodor Dostoevsky (D); Aug. 21: Søren Kierkegaard (D); Sept. 2: Grillparzer, Flaubert, Kleist, Dostoevsky (LF); Dec. 11: Kleist: "Michael Kohlhaas" (D); Dec. 14: Shaw, Dostoevsky (D).
1914	July–Dec.: *The Trial* Oct.: "In the Penal Colony" Dec.: "The Village Schoolteacher"	Jan. 5: Goethe (D); Jan. 6, Feb. 11: Wilhelm Dilthey (D); Jan. 12: Tolstoy (D); Feb. 14, March 13, April 15, May 12: Grillparzer: "Der arme Spielmann" (LF); Feb. 23: Robert Musil (D); March 15, May 29, June 12, Nov. 1, Dec. 20: Dostoevsky (D).
1915	Feb.: "Blumfeld, an Elderly Bachelor"	Jan. 17, March 23, May 4: Strindberg (D); Feb. 9: Flaubert: *Bouvard et Pécuchet* (D); March 3: Flaubert: *Letters* (LF); April 5, May 4: Strindberg (LF); May 6: Flaubert: *Salammbo* (LF); May 26: Heinrich Heine (LF); Oct. 20: Musil (L).
1916	Stories finally collected in *A Country Doctor* (1919), including "A Country Doctor," "A Report to an Academy," "In the Gallery," "A Fratricide," "The New Advocate," "Jackals and Arabs."	Aug. 27: Flaubert, Kierkegaard, Grillparzer (D); Oct. 26: Strindberg (LF); Dec. 14: Dickens: *Little Dorrit* (LF).

1917	Jan.–May: "The Hunter Gracchus" March–April: "The Great Wall of China "An Old Manuscript" Oct.: "A Common Confusion" "The Truth about Sancho Panza" "The Silence of the Sirens" Oct. until Feb. 1918: "Reflections on Sin, Suffering, Hope and the True Way"	Sept. 25: Flaubert (D); Oct. 8: Dickens: *David Copperfield*, Robert Walser (D); Oct. 12, Nov. 24: Thomas Mann (L); Oct. until April 1918: Kierkegaard (L), a recurrent subject of letters to Max Brod.
1918		Jan.: Buber, Tolstoy: *Diaries* (L); March: Freud (L).
1919	Nov.: "Letter to His Father"	
1920	Jan.–Feb.: *He* (aphorisms)	
1921	"First Sorrow"	March: Grillparzer, Theodor Fontane (L); Sept: Flaubert: *Diaries* (L); Oct.: Kleist (L); Oct. 19: Flaubert: *L'Education Sentimentale* (D); Dec. 20: Wilhelm Raabe (D); Dec. 23: Tolstoy: "The Death of Ivan Ilyich" (D).
1922	Jan.–Sept.: *The Castle* Spring: "A Hunger Artist" Summer: "Investigations of a Dog"	May 12: Buber (D); June: Nicolai Gogol (L); June 30: Strindberg (L); July 27: Goethe: *Faust*, Heine, Eduard Mörike, Theodor Storm (L); Dec.: Werfel: *Schweiger* (L); Dec. 18: Kierkegaard: *Either/Or* (D).
1923	"A Little Woman" "The Burrow"	Dec. 17: Musil (L).
1924	March: "Josephine the Singer, or the Mouse Folk"	March: Hamsun (L).

Bibliography: The Trial *in English*

This checklist offers a comprehensive listing of work on *The Trial* available in English, excluding unpublished dissertations. Items included in the present volume, as a whole or in part, are not listed here. Relevant articles in the following well-known collections of essays on Kafka are listed separately:

Flores, Angel, ed. *The Kafka Problem.* New York: New Directions, 1946.

Flores, Angel and Homer Swander, eds. *Franz Kafka Today.* Madison: Wisconsin University Press, 1958. Includes useful bibliography.

Full Kafka bibliographies are available only in German. The most recent, to which the present list is indebted, is by Peter U. Beicken: *Franz Kafka, eine kritische Einführung in die Forschung.* Frankfurt: Athenaion, 1974.

Anders, Gunter. *Franz Kafka*, translated by A. Steer and A. K. Thorlby. New York: Hillary House, 1960.

Arendt, Hannah. "Franz Kafka: A Revaluation," *Partisan Review* 11 (1944), 412–422.

Beck, Evelyn Torton. *Kafka and the Yiddish Theatre.* Madison: University of Wisconsin Press, 1971, pp. 154–171.

Beissner, Friedrich. "Kafka the Artist," in *Kafka. A Collection of Critical Essays*, edited by Ronald Gray. Englewood Cliffs: Prentice-Hall, Inc., 1962, pp. 15–31.

Benjamin, Walter. "Franz Kafka, on the Tenth Anniversary of his death," in Benjamin, *Illuminations*, translated by Harry Zohn, edited by Hannah Arendt. New York: Schocken Paperback, 1969, pp. 111–140. First published in *Jüdische Rundschau* 102 (1934).

Born, Jürgen. "Kafka's Parable 'Before the Law': Reflections towards a Positive Interpretation," *Mosaic* 3 (1970), 153–162.

Bryant, Jerry H. "The Delusion of Hope. Franz Kafka: *The Trial*," *Symposium* 23 (1969), 116–128.

Camus, Albert. "Hope and the Absurd in the Work of Franz Kafka," in *Kafka. A*

Collection of Critical Essays, edited by Ronald Gray. Englewood Cliffs: Prentice-Hall, Inc., 1962, pp. 147-155.

Canetti, Elias. *Kafka's Other Trial: The Letters to Felice*, translated by Christopher Middleton. New York: Schocken Books, 1974.

Church, Margaret. "Time and Reality in Kafka's *The Trial* and *The Castle*," *Twentieth-Century Literature* 2 (1956), 62-69.

Collins, R. G. "Kafka's Special Methods of Thinking," *Mosaic* 3 (1970), 43-57.

Dauvin, Rene. "*The Trial*. Its Meaning," in *Franz Kafka Today*, 145-160.

Deinert, Herbert. "Kafka's Parable 'Before the Law'," *Germanic Review* 39 (1964), no. 3, 192-200.

Diller, Edward. "Theonomous homiletics 'Vor dem Gesetz'. Franz Kafka and Paul Tillich," *Revue des Langues Vivantes* 36 (1970), 289-294.

Dyson, A. E. "Trial by Enigma. Kafka's *The Trial*," in Dyson, *Between Two Worlds*. New York: St. Martin's Press, 1972, pp. 114-134.

Feuerlicht, Ignace. "Discussions and Contradictions in Kafka's *Trial*," *German Quarterly* 40 (1967), no. 3, 339-350.

―――― "Kafka's Chaplain," *German Quarterly* 39 (1966), no. 2, 208-220.

―――― "Kafka's Joseph K.—A Man with Qualities," *Seminar* 3 (1967), no. 2, 103-116.

Fickert, Kurt J. "The Window Metaphor in Kafka's *Trial*," *Monatshefte*, 58 (1966), no. 4, 345-352.

Fort, Keith. "The Function of Style in Franz Kafka's *The Trial*," *Sewanee Review* 72 (1964), 643-651.

Foulkes, A. Peter. *The Reluctant Pessimist. A Study of Franz Kafka*. The Hague, Paris: Mouton, 1967, pp. 157-163.

Fromm, Erich. "Kafka's *The Trial*," in Fromm, *The Forgotten Language*. New York: Grove Press, 1957, pp. 249-263.

Gray, Ronald. *Franz Kafka*. Cambridge University Press, 1973, pp. 103-125.

Greenberg, Martin. *The Terror of Art. Kafka and Modern Literature*. New York: Basic Books, 1968, pp. 113-153.

Groethuysen, Bernhard. "The Endless Labyrinth," in *The Kafka Problem*, 376-390.

Gunwaldsen, Kaare M. "The Plot of Kafka's *Trial*," *Monatshefte* 56 (1964), no. 1, 1-14.

Handler, Gary. "A Note on the Structure of Kafka's *Der Prozess*," *Modern Language Notes* 84 (1969), 798-799.

Hoffman, Frederick J. "Kafka's *The Trial*: The Assailant as Landscape," *Bucknell Review* 9 (1960), 89–105.

Jaffe, Adrian H. *The Process of Kafka's Trial*. East Lansing: Michigan State University Press, 1967.

Kartiganer, Donald M. "Job and Josef K.: Myth in Kafka's *The Trial*," *Modern Fiction Studies* 8 (1962), no. 1, 31–43.

Kelly, John. "*The Trial* and the Theology of Crisis," in *The Kafka Problem*, 151–171.

Kudszus, Winfried. "Between Past and Future: Kafka's Later Novels," *Mosaic* 3 (1969/70), no. 4, 107–118.

Kuhn, Ira. "The Metamorphosis of *The Trial*," *Symposium* 26 (1972), no. 3, 226–241. On the dramatization by Gide and Barrault.

Kuna, Franz. *Franz Kafka: Literature as Corrective Punishment*. Bloomington: Indiana University Press, 1974, pp. 99–135.

Leon, R. St. "Religious Motives in Kafka's *Der Prozess*. Some Textual Notes," *Journal of the Australasian Universities Language and Literature Association* 19 (1963), 21–38.

Leopold, Keith. "Breaks in Perspective in Franz Kafka's *Der Prozess*," *German Quarterly* 36 (1963), no. 1, 31–38.

Lesser, Simon O. "The Source of Guilt and the Sense of Guilt—Kafka's *The Trial*," *Modern Fiction Studies* 8 (1962), no. 1, 44–60.

Levi, P. Margot. "K. An Exploration of the Names of Kafka's Central Characters," *Names* 14 (1966), no. 1, 1–10.

Lindsay, J. M. "Kohlhaas and K. Two Men in Search for Justice," *German Life and Letters* 13 (1959/60), no. 3, 190–194.

Lukacs, Georg. "Franz Kafka or Thomas Mann?" in Lukacs, *Realism in our Time*, translated by J. and N. Mander. New York: Harper and Row, 1964.

Marson, Eric L. "Justice and the Obsessed Character in *Michael Kohlhaas, Der Prozess* and *L'Étranger*," *Seminar* 2 (1966), no. 2, 21–33.

———, *Kafka's 'The Trial': The Case against Josef K*. St. Lucia, Australia: University of Queensland Press, 1975.

Mellen, Joan. "Joseph K. and the Law," *Texas Studies in Literature and Language* 12 (1970/71), 295–302.

Neider, Charles. *The Frozen Sea*. New York: Oxford University Press, 1948, pp. 153–180.

Pasley, Malcolm. "Two Literary Sources of Kafka's *Der Prozess*," *Forum for Modern Language Studies* 3 (1967), 142–147.

Politzer, Heinz. *Franz Kafka. Parable and Paradox.* Ithaca, New York: Cornell University Press, 1962, second edition 1966, pp. 163–217.

———, "The Puzzle of Kafka's Prosecuting Attorney," *Publications of the Modern Language Association* 75 (1960), no. 4, 432–438.

Purdy, Strother B. "Religion and Death in Kafka's *Der Prozess*," *Papers on Language and Literature* 5 (1969), 170–182.

Rahv, Philip. "The Death of Ivan Ilyich and Joseph K.," in Rahv, *Image and Idea*. New York: New Directions, 1949, pp. 111–127.

Reed, Eugene E. "Moral Polarity in Franz Kafka's *Der Prozess* and *Das Schloss*," *Monatshefte* 46 (1954), no. 6, 317–324.

Rhein, Philip H. *The Urge to Live. A Comparative Study of Franz Kafka's Der Prozess and Albert Camus' L'Étranger.* Chapel Hill: University of North Carolina Press, 1964.

Rolleston, James. *Kafka's Narrative Theater.* University Park: Pennsylvania State University Press, 1974, pp. 69–87.

Spaini, Alberto. "The Trial," in *The Kafka Problem*, 143–150.

Spiro, Solomon J. "Verdict—Guilty: A Study of *The Trial*," *Twentieth Century Literature* 17 (1971), 169–179.

Stern, J. P. "Franz Kafka. The Labyrinth of Guilt," *Critical Quarterly* 7 (1965), no. 1, 35–47.

Szanto, George H. *Narrative Consciousness: Structure and Perspective in the Fiction of Kafka, Beckett and Robbe-Grillet.* Austin: University of Texas Press, 1972, pp. 17–40.

Tauber, Herbert. *Franz Kafka: An Interpretation of His Works*, translated by G. Humphreys Roberts and Roger Senhouse. New Haven: Yale University Press, 1948, pp. 77–120.

Thorlby, Anthony. *Kafka: A Study.* London: Heinemann, 1972, pp. 53–68.

Uyttersprot, Herman. "*The Trial.* Its Structure," in *Franz Kafka Today*, 127–144.

Vallette, Rebecca M. "*Der Prozess* and *Le Procès*: A Study in Dramatic Adaptation," *Modern Drama* 10 (1967), 87–94.

Waldmeir, Joseph J. "Anti-Semitism as an Issue in The Trial of Kafka's Josef K.," *Books Abroad* 35 (1961), 10–15.

Webster, Peter Dow. "Arrested Individuation or the Problem of Josef K. and Hamlet," *American Imago* 5 (1948), no. 3, 225–245.

Wilson, A. K. "Null and Void. An Interpretation of the Significance of the Court in Franz Kafka's *Der Prozess*," *German Life and Letters* 14 (1960/61), no. 3, 165–169.

Ziolkowski, Theodore. "Franz Kafka: *The Trial*," in Ziolkowski, *Dimensions of the Modern Novel. German Texts and European Contexts*. Princeton: Princeton University Press, 1967, pp. 37–67.

Other Twentieth Century Interpretations Books

Maynard Mack, Series Editor

AS YOU LIKE IT, Halio, J. (Ed.)
OLD MAN AND THE SEA, THE, Jobes, K. (Ed.)
FALL OF THE HOUSE OF USHER, THE, Woodson, T. (Ed.)
BEGGAR'S OPERA, THE, Noble, Y. (Ed.)
CORIOLANUS, Phillips, J. (Ed.)
CASTLE, THE, Neumeyer, P.
FAREWELL TO ARMS, A, Gellens, J. (Ed.)
NINETEEN HUNDRED EIGHTY-FOUR (1984), Hynes, S. (Ed.)
GRAY'S ELEGY, Starr, H. (Ed.)
LORD JIM, Kuehn, R. (Ed.)
PRIDE AND PREJUDICE, Rubinstein, E. (Ed.)
ABSALOM, ABSALOM!, Goldman, A.
COLLECTION OF CRITICAL ESSAYS ON "THE WASTE LAND", A, Martin, J. (Ed.)
GULLIVER'S TRAVELS, Brady, F. (Ed.)
MOLL FLANDERS, Elliott, R. (Ed.)
OEDIPUS REX, O'Brien, M. (Ed.)
BILLY BUDD, Vincent, H. (Ed.)
MEASURE FOR MEASURE, Geckle, G. (Ed.)
MOLLOY, MALONE DIES, THE UNNAMABLE, O'Hara, J. (Ed.)
BLEAK HOUSE, Korg, J. (Ed.)
CRUCIBLE, THE, Ferres, J. (Ed.)
EVE OF SAINT AGNES, THE, Danzig, A. (Ed.)
HAMLET, Bevington, D. (Ed.)

ICEMAN COMETH, THE, Raleigh, J. (Ed.)
GREAT GATSBY, THE, Lockridge, E. (Ed.)
MAJOR BARBARA, Zimbardo, R. (Ed.)
MISS LONELYHEARTS, Jackson, T. (Ed.)
WALDEN, Ruland, R. (Ed.)
ARROWSMITH, Griffin, R. (Ed.)
MERCHANT OF VENICE, THE, Barnet, S. (Ed.)
STREETCAR NAMED DESIRE, A, Miller, J. (Ed.)
UTOPIA, Nelson, W. (Ed.)
VANITY FAIR, Sundell, M. (Ed.)
CRIME AND PUNISHMENT, Jackson, R. (Ed.)
HARD TIMES, Gray, P. (Ed.)
BOOK OF JOB, THE, Sanders, P. (Ed.)
MUCH ADO ABOUT NOTHING, Davis, W. (Ed.)
ADVENTURES OF HUCKLEBERRY FINN, THE, Simpson, C. (Ed.)
MURDER IN THE CATHEDRAL, Clark, D. (Ed.)
PLAYBOY OF THE WESTERN WORLD, THE, Whitaker, T. (Ed.)
POE'S TALES, Howarth, W. (Ed.)
RICHARD II, Cubeta, P. (Ed.)
RIME OF THE ANCIENT MARINER, THE, Boulger, J. (Ed.)
BOSWELL'S LIFE OF JOHNSON, Clifford, J. (Ed.)
ROBINSON CRUESOE, Ellis, F. (Ed.)
PARDONER'S TALE, THE, Faulkner, D. (Ed.)
PASSAGE TO INDIA, A, Rutherford, A. (Ed.)
ROMEO AND JULIET, Cole, D. (Ed.)
TALE OF TWO CITIES, A, Beckwith, C. (Ed.)
INVISIBLE MAN, Reilly, J. (Ed.)
HENRY IV, PART I, Dorius, R. (Ed.)
HENRY IV, PART II, Young, D. (Ed.)
RAINBOW, THE, Kinkead-Weekes, M. (Ed.)
SAMSON AGONISTES, Crump, G. (Ed.)
RAPE OF THE LOCK, THE, Rousseau, G. (Ed.)
WOMEN IN LOVE, Miko, S. (Ed.)

ALL FOR LOVE, King, B. (Ed.)
HENRY V, Berman, R. (Ed.)
AMBASSADORS, THE, Stone, A. Jr. (Ed.)
NATIVE SON, Baker, H. Jr.
SCARLET LETTER, THE, Gerber, J. (Ed.)
TEMPEST, THE, Smith, H. (Ed.)
LIGHT IN AUGUST, Minter, D. (Ed.)
PORTRAIT OF THE ARTIST AS A YOUNG MAN, A, Schutte, W. (Ed.)
WUTHERING HEIGHTS, Vogler, T. (Ed.)
DON JUAN, Bostetter, E. (Ed.)
JULIUS CAESAR, Dean, L. (Ed.)
SIR GAWAIN AND THE GREEN KNIGHT, Fox, D. (Ed.)
DUBLINERS, Garrett, P. (Ed.)
DUCHESS OF MALFI, THE, Rabkin, N. (Ed.)
KEATS' ODES, Stillinger, J. (Ed.)
TO THE LIGHTHOUSE, Volger, T. (Ed.)
TOM JONES, Battestin, M. (Ed.)
SONGS OF INNOCENCE AND EXPERIENCE, Paley, M. (Ed.)
SONS AND LOVERS, Farr, J. (Ed.)
SOUND AND THE FURY, THE, Cowan, M. (Ed.)
TURN OF THE SCREW AND OTHER TALES, THE, Tompkins, J. (Ed.)
TWELFTH NIGHT, King, W. (Ed.)
ENDGAME, Chevigny, B. (Ed.)